McKinley Bibliographies

Volume 1

A GUIDE TO HISTORICAL FICTION

For the Use of Schools,
Libraries and the General Reader

Compiled by
LEONARD B. IRWIN

TENTH EDITION
New and Revised

Brooklawn, N. J.
McKinley Publishing Co.
1971

TABLE OF CONTENTS

TABLE OF CONTENTS

THE UNITED STATES

CANADA AND LATIN AMERICA

PREFACE

The late Hannah Logasa inaugurated the *Historical Fiction* volume in the McKinley series of bibliographies, and carried it through a number of editions. The compiler of the present volume seeks to continue the purpose of the work, and hopes, through a number of changes in content, format and selectivity, to make it even more useful to teachers, librarians and the public.

Leonard B. Irwin

INTRODUCTION

A bibliographical guide to historical novels obviously has only one chief purpose — that of assisting librarians, teachers and the general reader in identifying books that will meet their particular needs. The present compiler believes this guide will achieve such a goal through the descriptive annotation that accompanies each title, and through the selective process that determined what titles should be included. It should be understood that the *Guide* is not an exhaustive list of all historical novels ever published. Rather, it has two selective factors: first, no books have been included that were not well received by critics and the public at the time of publication; second, in general only books published since 1940 have been listed. There are a few notable exceptions to this last limitation, since there are a number of outstanding historical novels written earlier in the century which are just as popular and readable today as ever. Some of these have been listed, admittedly largely on the basis of the compiler's own preferences.

The definition, nature and value of historical fiction have been subject to endless debate and discussion. What is an historical novel? In one sense almost any novel, no matter how contemporary, could be said to become an historical novel as soon as it is published, if it reflects accurately a particular time and set of human conditions. But this is too broad for practical purposes and ordinary usage. Therefore this *Guide* has tried to follow three criteria: that the setting of the novel is a period of time earlier than that in which the author does his writing; that the plot and characters should accurately reflect that period and background as they were; and that the story should depend for its value chiefly for having been set in a particular time and place in the past.

The nature and value of historical fiction can, of course, vary greatly. Such novels can range from the simply sensational items, such as *Forever Amber,* through the swashbuckling adventure tales of writers like Sabatini and Van Wyck Mason, to literary classics like *Giants in the Earth* or *Johnny Tremaine.* There are devotees of historical fiction, just as there are mystery story fans; and there are others who sneer at historical novels as pablum for those unable to take their history straight. It is certainly a matter of taste. A cheap novel, using an historical background merely as a colorful rack on which to hang a shoddy story, has little to be said for it. But a well-written novel, using its period setting as an integral and necessary means of developing its characters and plot, can be a literary masterpiece; and it can also provide its readers with a sense of historical understanding and realism that otherwise would be denied to all but the professional scholar.

It would seem very likely that the young student who is encouraged to read stories set in a past day is going to be more receptive to reading serious history because of it. Past generations who grew up with Howard Pyle, G. A. Henty or Mary Johnston certainly acquired at least a sympathetic curiosity about history; and today's young people are equally influenced by more modern story-tellers. Good historical fiction cannot replace good historical research and writing, but it can provide a predisposition for it as well as a pleasurable supplement to it. Most of the novels listed in this volume are notable for the serious and careful research which the authors provide for their backgrounds. Writing a good historical novel cannot be done off the cuff. Too many errors and anachronisms are sure to occur.

Many good historical tales have been written for young people not yet quite ready for adult fiction. Lists of these have been provided at the end of each section of the book, and will be appropriate for the average reader aged from about 12 to 15.

No attempt has been made to indicate which titles were in print at the time of publication of the *Guide*. This is a factor which changes rapidly in the publishing field, especially because of the great influence of paperbacks; and many titles which went out of print as hard cover editions have returned to the market as paperbacks. This trend will certainly continue.

No book of this kind can be kept entirely free of errors, but the compiler hopes he has kept them to a minimum in quantity or importance. He hopes also that the book will meet the needs of those for whom it is intended, and particularly that it will help young people to an appreciation and love of history.

THE ANCIENT WORLD

EGYPT AND MESOPOTAMIA

Bauer, Florence. *Abram, son of Terah.* **Bobbs, 1948.**
Set in the city of Ur, this is a good story of the times and early life of Abram.

Fast, Howard. *Moses, prince of Egypt.* **Crown, 1958.**
Colorful and well-written story of the young manhood of Moses.

Grant, Joan. *Winged pharaoh.* **Harper, 1938.**
A good novel depicting the life and religious beliefs of Egypt sixty centuries ago, through the life of a daughter of the Pharaoh.

Hall, Arthur D. *Golden balance.* **Crown, 1955.**
A novel of ancient Egypt of the 15th century B.C., telling how a clever boy became a court favorite, leading to eventual disaster.

Hardy, William. *All the trumpets sounded.* **Coward, 1942.**
Long but well-written novel about the life of Moses.

Hawkes, Jacquetta. *King of the two lands.* **Random, 1966.**
Set in ancient Egypt in the time of Akhenaten and Nefertiti.

McGraw, Eloise. *Pharaoh.* **Coward, 1958.**
Interesting and colorful novel about Hatshepsut, the queen who proclaimed herself pharaoh until her growing son took his rightful power from her.

Waltari, Mika. *The Egyptian.* **Putnam, 1949.**
An exceptional story of an Egyptian physician in about 1000 B.C., whose career touches many facets of society and experience.

Wilson, Dorothy. *Prince of Egypt.* **Westminster, 1949.**
A long, graphic novel of the life of Moses up to the period of the Exodus.

1

JUVENILE

Baumann, Hans. *World of the pharaohs.* **Pantheon, 1960.**
Story of a boy travelling in Egypt with his father, an archaeologist, and thereby learning a great deal about the ancient land.

Coolidge, Olivia. *Egyptian adventures.* **Houghton, 1953.**
Contains twelve good short stories about various phases of ancient Egyptian society.

Fyson, Jennifer G. *The three brothers of Ur.* **Coward, 1966.**
Story of three boys in ancient Mesopotamia, with good portrayal of religious and cultural life.

McGraw, Eloise. *Golden goblet.* **Coward, 1961.**
Set in ancient Egypt, a story of a stolen cup, and of a well-portrayed boy. The craft of the goldsmith and other backgrounds are realistic.

McGraw, Eloise. *Mara, daughter of the Nile.* **Coward, 1953.**
Excitement, espionage and romance in a good story of ancient Egypt.

Morrison, Lucille. *Lost queen of Egypt.* **Stokes, 1937.**
Very careful and authentic background for this story about the daughter of Akhenaten and Nefertiti.

Noble, Iris. *Egypt's Queen Cleopatra.* **Messner, 1963.**
Actually a fictionalized biography derived chiefly from Plutarch.

GREECE

Anderson, Florence. *Black sail.* **Crown, 1948.**
Well-written version of the myth of Theseus and the Minotaur.

Baker, George E. *Paris of Troy.* **Ziff-Davis, 1947.**
This is a story of the siege of Troy, and makes normal, interesting people out of the famous names from legend.

De Camp, Lyon. *Bronze god of Rhodes.* **Doubleday, 1959.**
Good novel with authentic background about Chares, who built the
Colossus of Rhodes.

De Camp, Lyon. *Elephant for Aristotle.* **Doubleday, 1958.**
Humorous and colorful story of how Alexander the Great sent an
elephant from India to Athens as a gift to his old tutor, Aristotle.

Druon, Maurice. *Alexander the god.* **Scribner, 1961.**
Novel based on the life and conquests of Alexander the Great, and
on his belief that he was a descendant of Zeus.

Duggan, Alfred. *Besieger of cities.* **Pantheon, 1963.**
Novel about Demetrius, the Macedonian who spent his life trying
to restore Alexander's empire. Realistic picture of warfare and
society of the 3rd century B.C.

Eiker, Karl V. *Star of Macedon.* **Putnam, 1957.**
An unflattering picture of Alexander the Great as narrated by one
of his slaves.

Graves, Robert. *Hercules, my shipmate.* **Creative Age, 1945.**
An epic and lusty telling of the story of Jason and the Argonauts, as
though it were history rather than legend. Excellent writing.

Graves, Robert. *Homer's daughter.* **Doubleday, 1955.**
Very well-written novel about the legends of Nausicaa.

Green, Peter. *The laughter of Aphrodite.* **Doubleday, 1965.**
Fictional biography of Sappho, the poetess of ancient Lesbos. Good
re-creation of a woman of whom little is really known.

Hansen, Eva. *Scandal in Troy.* **Random, 1956.**
Light-hearted re-telling of the story of Helen of Troy.

3

Johnson, Eyvind. *Return to Ithaca.* **Thames, 1952.**
The story of the Odyssey retold in modern novel form.

Marlowe, Stephen. *The shining.* **Trident, 1963.**
A novel of ancient Greece, in which the principal character is the controversial Alcibiades.

Menen, Aubrey. *A conspiracy of women.* **Random, 1965.**
The Macedonian women who followed Alexander's army into Persia are outraged when he orders his men to take Persian wives.

Payne, Robert. *Alexander the god.* **Wyn, 1954.**
Fictional portrait of Alexander the Great and his career.

Penfield, Wilder. *The torch.* **Little, 1960.**
Written with authentic realism, this is a story about Hippocrates and the healing arts in ancient Greece.

Pick, Robert. *Escape of Socrates.* **Knopf, 1954.**
A modern version in fiction form of the life of Socrates and the Athenian scene.

Poole, Lynn and Gray. *Magnificent traitor.* **Dodd, 1968.**
Excellent novel of the career of Alcibiades and of the world of Athens in the time of Pericles.

Powell, Richard. *Whom the gods would destroy.* **Scribner, 1970.**
Good novel about the Trojan War. While a boy is the central figure, nearly all the classic Homeric characters take their parts.

Renault, Mary. *Fire from heaven.* **Pantheon, 1969.**
Fine novel about the youth of Alexander prior to his succeeding to the throne of Macedon.

Renault, Mary. *The king must die.* Pantheon, 1958.
The Greek myths about Theseus are the material for this novel, and Theseus himself is the narrator.

Renault, Mary. *The last of the wine.* Pantheon, 1956.
Excellent novel of life and exciting events in the Athens of Socrates. Unusually good realism.

Renault, Mary. *Mask of Apollo.* Pantheon, 1966.
Set in ancient Syracuse and Athens in the 4th century, B.C., it depicts the drama and philosophical conflicts of that period.

Stewart, George R. *Years of the city.* Houghton, 1955.
A long solidly written story of the founding, growth and downfall of an imaginary Greek city.

Sutcliff, Rosemary. *Flowers of Adonis.* Coward, 1970.
Novel about Alcibiades, the Greek general, told by a number of his fellow-citizens of varied types.

Treece, Henry. *Amber princess.* Random, 1963.
Melodramatic and violent retelling of the myths of Electra, Helen, Orestes, Clytemnestra and Agamemnon.

Treece, Henry. *Jason.* Random, 1961.
Novel based on the myth of the Argonauts, with a competent and realistic setting.

Warner, Rex. *Pericles the Athenian.* Little, 1963.
Re-creation of the city of Athens and its citizens in the 5th century B.C., vividly done.

5

JUVENILE

Andrews, Mary. *Hostage to Alexander.* **Longmans, 1961.**
A boy becomes a follower of the conqueror in his campaigns. Good
historical background.

Coolidge, Olivia. *The king of men.* **Houghton, 1966.**
Excellent novel based on the Agamemnon legend and other Homeric
myths.

Efremov, Ivan. *Land of foam.* **Houghton, 1959.**
The first story for young people to be translated from Russian into
English. About a young sculptor in ancient Greece who travels
through Africa after escaping from slavers. Excellent picture of
ancient Africa.

Faulkner, Nancy. *Traitor queen.* **Doubleday, 1963.**
Story of a girl in the court of King Minos of Crete who becomes
involved in a treacherous plot of the queen, who comes from Mycena.

Ingles, James. *Test of valor.* **Westminster, 1953.**
Story about a young Greek athlete taking part in the ancient
Olympics.

Johnson, Dorothy M. *Farewell to Troy.* **Houghton, 1964.**
Recounts the fall of Troy and what happened afterward as it might
have been seen by the young grandson of King Priam.

Lawrence, Isabelle. *Niko: sculptor's apprentice.* **Viking, 1956.**
Story about a boy in ancient Athens who is apprenticed to Phidias
during the construction of the Parthenon.

Plowman, Stephanie. *Road to Sardis.* **Houghton, 1966.**
About a boy in the days of the wars between Athens and Sparta,
who grows up to see the defeat and corruption of Athens.

Ray, Mary. *The voice of Apollo.* **Farrar, 1965.**
Story of a boy in Delphi of the 6th century B.C. and how he became involved in the destruction of the temple of Apollo.

Snedeker, Caroline. *Lysis goes to the play.* **Lothrop, 1962.**
Story of two children attending a new play by Euripides on the Acropolis.

Sprague, Rosemary. *Northward to Albion.* **Roy, 1947.**
The legend of Bruttys, great-grandson of Aeneas, who is supposed to have led the first settlers to Britain.

Williamson, T. R. *Before Homer.* **Longmans, 1938.**
Story of two boys in ancient Greece.

ROME

Atherton, Gertrude. *Golden peacock.* **Houghton, 1936.**
A novel about Augustan Rome, in which a young woman discovers a plot against Augustus. Vivid portrayal of Imperial Rome.

Baron, Alexander. *Queen of the East.* **Washburn, 1956.**
Full of action, panoply and color, a novel about the conflict between Queen Zenobia of Palmyra and the Roman Emperor Aurelian.

Bryher. *The coin of Carthage.* **Harcourt, 1963.**
Interesting story about two Greek traders in Hannibal's time just after the Second Punic War. Their adventures take them into both Rome and Carthage.

Bryher. *Roman wall.* **Pantheon, 1954.**
Well-written novel of a Roman outpost which is eventually overrun by a barbarian tribe.

Costain, Thomas B. *Darkness and the dawn.* **Doubleday, 1959.**
Romance and adventure in a vigorous story of Attila the Hun's invasion of 5th century Europe.

7

Costain, Thomas B. *Silver chalice.* **Doubleday, 1952.**
Gripping and highly colorful novel about the Holy Grail, against the background of early Christianity in Rome and Palestine.

Crozier, William. *The fates are laughing.* **Harcourt, 1945.**
Based on long research, a fine novel of ancient Rome in the days of Tiberius and the early Christians.

De Wohl, Louis. *Citadel of God.* **Lippincott, 1959.**
Colorful novel about the life and work of St. Benedict, and about Rome under the Goths.

De Wohl, Louis. *Imperial renegade.* **Lippincott, 1949.**
Fourth century Roman Empire and the career of Julian the Apostate, who tried to restrain the growth of Christianity. Colorful, graphic, sometimes brutal.

Dolan, Mary. *Hannibal of Carthage.* **Macmillan, 1955.**
A novel based on Hannibal's career, bringing out the many qualities of his actual greatness. Unusually well done.

Duggan, Alfred. *Children of the wolf.* **Coward, 1959.**
Excellent story of the founding of Rome and the transition from savagery to civilization. Figures from several places — Greece, Etruria, etc. — are chief characters.

Duggan, Alfred. *Family favorites.* **Pantheon, 1960.**
Story about the teen-age Roman Emperor Heliogabalus, as purportedly told by a Gallic member of his guard. An excellent recreation.

Duggan, Alfred. *Three's company.* **Coward, 1957.**
Story about Rome's First Triumvirate, but particularly its least-known member, Lepidus. Well-written, authentic background.

Duggan, Alfred. *Winter quarters.* **Coward, 1956.**
Good evocation of the almost mythological past of ancient Rome and Syria.

Ellert, Gerhart. *Gregory the Great.* **Harcourt, 1963.**
Novel based on the career of Gregory Anicius, the 6th century
pope and saint.

Feuchtwanger, Lion. *Josephus and the emperor.* **Viking, 1942.**
Dramatic novel of the later years of the Jewish historian Josephus,
and of Rome under Domitian. This is the third of the author's
trilogy of novels about Josephus.

Fisher, Ed Z. *Wine, women and woad.* **Macmillan, 1960.**
An amusing satirical novel about decadent Rome, as it might have
been had it had modern problems and politicians.

Gerard, Francis. *Scarlet beast.* **Longmans, 1934.**
Adventure story of the Second Punic War and Hannibal's attack
on Rome.

Gibson, John. *Patrician street.* **Vanguard, 1940.**
Realistic picture of decadent Rome during the time of Christian
persecution.

Graves, Ralph. *The lost eagles.* **Knopf, 1955.**
Adventure story of the period of the Emperor Augustus. A young
man undertakes to recover three golden eagles which German barbarians had captured from the Roman standards.

Green, Peter. *Sword of pleasure.* **World, 1958.**
Novel based on the life of Lucius Cornelius Sulla, Roman dictator.

Hardy, William G. *City of libertines.* **Appleton, 1957.**
Authentic historical settings in this novel about Rome in the time
of Caesar and Catullus the poet.

Horia, Vintila. *God was born in exile.* **St. Martins, 1961.**
About the Roman poet Ovid, banished in 9 A.D. to exile in a small
town on the Black Sea.

9

James, John. *Votan.* **New Am. Lib., 1967.**
Second century A.D. on the Danube borders of the Roman Empire.
Exploits and adventures of a Greek hero, Photinus. Good reading.

Koch, Werner. *Pontius Pilate reflects.* **Simon & Schuster, 1962.**
Pilate, a broken and disgraced man, spends his last years in reflection about the past.

Koestler, Arthur. *The gladiators.* **Macmillan, 1939.**
Panoramic story of Rome shortly before the rise of Julius Caesar.
Spartacus and the revolt of the gladiators are the central theme.

Mabie, Mary. *Prepare them for Caesar.* **Little, 1949.**
An admiring picture of the adult life of Julius Caesar, and a vivid one of Roman life in the first century B.C.

Maier, Paul L. *Pontius Pilate.* **Doubleday, 1968.**
Shows the beginnings of Christianity in a novel well-researched and using only historical characters. Good history with a fictional facade.

Powers, Anne. *No king but Caesar.* **Doubleday, 1960.**
Romance and intrigue in the Rome of Caligula.

Raynolds, Robert. *Sinner of Saint Ambrose.* **Bobbs, 1952.**
Fictional portrayal of the last days of the Roman Empire, giving the reader an understanding of those momentous times.

Samuel, Maurice. *The second crucifixion.* **Knopf, 1960.**
About a 2nd century Jewish girl who leaves her Roman husband and joins the Jewish community in Rome. The "second crucifixion" is the bitter anti-Semitism that has grown up.

Saylor, Carol. *The equinox.* **Lippincott, 1966.**
Intrigue and melodrama in the reign of the Roman Emperor Commodus.

Siegel, Benjamin. *Sword and the promise.* **Harcourt, 1959.**
Set in the 2nd century Roman world of Hadrian, this is an adventurous tale about a young Greek physician. Action and color.

Slaughter, Frank G. *Constantine.* **Doubleday, 1965.**
A novel about Rome's first Christian emperor. Violent action and excellent background material.

Solon, Gregory. *Three legions.* **Random, 1956.**
Story of the disintegration of Roman legions in the endless fight against the barbarians.

Taylor, Anna. *The gods are not mocked.* **Morrow, 1969.**
A novel set in the period of Caesar's invasion of Britain. Numerous interesting characters and realistic background.

Treece, Henry. *Dark Island.* **Random, 1953.**
About the Roman defeat of the Celtic tribes in first-century Britain.

Vidal, Gore. *Julian.* **Little, 1964.**
Novel based on the 4th century Roman Emperor, Julian the Apostate.

Wagner, John and Esther. *Gift of Rome.* **Little, 1961.**
Good picture of ancient Rome in a story about an important legal trial in which Cicero defends a man unjustly accused of murder.

Warner, Rex. *The converts.* **Little, 1967.**
Fourth century Rome and the conversion of Augustine to Christianity.

Warner, Rex. *Imperial Caesar.* **Little, 1960.**
A fictional tour-de-force, this represents Caesar's recollections of fifteen years as he lies sleepless the night before the fatal visit to the Senate.

11

White, Helen C. *Four rivers of paradise.* **Macmillan, 1955.**
The story of a young man who visits decadent Rome during the
conquest by Alaric. He returns to France to try to preach Christianity to the barbarians.

Wilder, Thornton. *Ides of March.* **Harper, 1948.**
Highly interesting and clever portrayal of Caesar and the Roman
scene in 45 B. C. A fiction classic.

Yourcenar, Marguerite. *Memoirs of Hadrian.* **Farrar, 1954.**
Masterly novel about the life of Hadrian, full of realism and vivid
authenticity.

JUVENILE

Anderson, Paul L. *Swords in the north.* **Appleton, 1935.**
A story of Caesar's conquest of Britain and the years that followed,
exciting and with good background.

Behn, Harry. *Omen of the birds.* **World, 1964.**
A charming romance set in the period of Etruscan domination of
early Rome.

Gale, Elizabeth. *Julia Valeria.* **Putnam, 1951.**
Romantic story for girls in the period of Augustan Rome.

Houghton, Eric. *The white wall.* **McGraw, 1962.**
A boy's adventures as a member of Hannibal's march across the
Alps to Rome.

Llewellyn, Richard. *Flame of Hercules.* **Doubleday, 1955.**
About a young fugitive galley slave in the first century A.D. Vivid
picture of ancient Rome and of the destruction of Pompeii.

Merrell, Leigh. *Prisoners of Hannibal.* **Nelson, 1958.**
A young Roman nobleman is captured by Hannibal during the
Second Punic War, and plots an escape.

Sutcliff, Rosemary. *The eagle of the ninth.* **Walck, 1954.**
Good story about a young Roman in occupied Britain.

Sutcliff, Rosemary. *The mark of the Horse Lord.* **Walck, 1965.**
Excellent and exciting story of a boy trained as a gladiator in Roman-occupied Britain, and his many adventures.

Sutcliff, Rosemary. *The silver branch.* **Oxford U.P., 1958.**
Dramatic and realistic tale about the Romans in Britain.

Trease, Geoffrey. *Message to Hadrian.* **Vanguard, 1956.**
About a young British traveler to Rome in the days of the Emperor Hadrian.

Treece, Henry. *Queen's brooch.* **Putnam, 1967.**
Story of a young Roman officer in Britain, involved in the revolt of Boadicea.

Treece, Henry. *War dog.* **Criterion, 1963.**
Britain during Caesar's conquest in 55 B.C. and a boy's story about a dog.

Williamson, Joanne. *The iron charm.* **Knopf, 1963.**
Exciting and far-ranging adventures of a young 6th century Roman, from the Constantinople of Justinian to the Britain of Arthur.

PALESTINE AND THE NEAR EAST

Asch, Shalom, *Mary.* **Putnam, 1949.**
The third in Asch's trilogy of fine novels about the beginning of the Christian faith. This covers the period of Jesus' life.

Asch, Shalom. *Moses.* **Putnam, 1951.**
A remarkable novel about the period of the Hebrew Exodus from Egypt.

13

Asch, Shalom. *The prophet.* **Putnam, 1955.**
One of this author's series of Biblical novels, this one centers on the prophet Isaiah and gives a vivid picture of his times and influence.

Bauer, Florence. *Behold your king.* **Bobbs, 1945.**
Authentic background setting in a novel of the last years of Jesus' life.

Bekessy, Emery. *Barabbas.* **Prentice, 1946.**
Novel about the people and stresses in Jerusalem at the time of Christ, reaching a strong climax in the scenes of the crucifixion.

Bercovici, Konrad. *The exodus.* **Beechhurst Press, 1947.**
A superior Biblical novel, dealing with the journey of the Israelites out of Egypt, and especially with Moses as their leader.

Blythe, LeGette. *Tear for Judas.* **Bobbs, 1951.**
A story of the time of Christ, in which Judas Iscariot is a central figure.

Brooker, Bertram. *The robber.* **Duell, 1949.**
An absorbing novel of the time of Jesus, in which Barabbas, Joseph of Arimathea and Judas are central figures.

Buckmaster, Henrietta. *And walk in love.* **Random, 1956.**
Excellent novel based on the life of St. Paul. Strong in historical background and characterization.

Cabries, Jean. *Jacob.* **Dutton, 1958.**
A long and powerful novel about Jacob's life from his deceiving of Isaac through the 21 years until he becomes Israel, the chosen of God.

Caldwell, Taylor. *Dear and glorious physician.* **Doubleday, 1958.**
Long and colorful novel about the life and times of St. Luke.

Chinn, Laurene. *The unanointed.* **Crown, 1958.**
A well-written novel about King David and Joab, his faithful follower.

De Ropp, Robert. *If I forget thee.* **St. Martins, 1956.**
Light melodramatic novel about Judea in 66 A.D. as the Jewish revolt against Roman rule began.

De Wohl, Louis. *Glorious folly.* **Lippincott, 1957.**
Novel based on the life and times of St. Paul.

Douglas, Lloyd. *The big fisherman.* **Houghton, 1948.**
Popular re-telling of the years of Jesus' ministry and of his disciples.

Dunscomb, Charles. *Bond and the free.* **Houghton, 1955.**
This well-written novel is in the form of letters written by a young Roman woman, the niece of Pontius Pilate. She is visiting in Jerusalem at the time of Jesus' trial. Vivid and realistic.

Fast, Howard. *Agrippa's daughter.* **Doubleday, 1964.**
Story of the daughter of Herod the Great and her husband during the destruction of Jerusalem by Titus, and the bitter conflicts of Jewish sects.

Fast, Howard. *My glorious brothers.* **Little, 1948.**
A novel of Israel in the time of the Maccabees, a century before Christ.

Feuchtwanger, Lion. *Jephtha and his daughter.* **Putnam, 1958.**
Powerful fictional telling of the Biblical story of the Israelite leader.

Feuchtwanger, Lion. *Josephus and the emperor.* **Viking, 1942.**
The third volume of the author's trilogy of novels about the Jewish historian.

Fineman, Irving. *Ruth.* **Harper, 1949.**
A fictionalized interpretation of the Biblical story of Ruth and Naomi.

Fisher, Vardis. *Island of the innocent.* **Abelard, 1952.**
A novel about conflict between Greek religious beliefs and Jewish monotheism at the time of the wars of the Maccabees. Colorful picture of the Near East about the third century B.C.

Fox, Paul. *Daughter of Jairus.* **Little, 1951.**
A religious novel, set in 1st century Judea and centering on the miracle of Christ's raising the daughter of Jairus from the dead.

Frieberger, Kurt. *Fisher of men.* **Appleton, 1954.**
Biographical novel about the life of Simon Peter.

Gann, Ernest K. *The antagonists.* **Simon & Schuster, 1970.**
A novel about the heroic defense of the heights of Masada by 900 Jews against the power of Rome in 73 A.D.

Hesky, Olga. *Painted queen.* **Obolensky, 1961.**
Biographical novel about Jezebel, Queen of Israel, in which she is pictured in a much more favorable light than tradition provides.

Ingles, James. *Woman of Samaria.* **Longmans, 1949.**
Well-written story about the life of Photina, and an excellent picture of Samaria in Christ's time.

Israel, Charles. *Rizpah.* **Simon & Schuster, 1961.**
Long and colorful story set in the days of Saul, David and Samuel about the girl who, having been captured by Philistines and rescued by Saul, marries him.

Kellner, Esther. *Mary of Nazareth.* **Appleton, 1958.**
Well-written and sensitive portrayal of Mary and the times of Jesus.

Kellner, Esther. *The promise.* **Westminster, 1956.**
The story of Abraham and Sarah in their long journey from Ur toward the promised land.

16

Lagerkvist, Par. *Herod and Mariamne.* **Knopf, 1968.**
A poignant love story of King Herod, the tyrant, representing the evils of mankind, and the spiritual woman who pities him and seeks to redeem him.

Linklater, Eric. *Husband of Delilah.* **Harcourt, 1962.**
Interesting novel of ancient Palestine, in which Samson and Delilah become real and human characters in a believable setting.

Maier, Paul L. *Pontius Pilate.* **Doubleday, 1968.**
A novel about Pilate's life, and the reasons for his momentous decision about Jesus.

Mann, Thomas. *Joseph, the provider.* **Knopf, 1944.**
The last of Mann's great series of novels about Joseph.

McGerr, Patricia. *Martha, Martha.* **Kenedy, 1960.**
Story about St. Martha of Bethany, the friend of Jesus.

Meisels, Andrew. *Son of a star.* **Putnam, 1969.**
Story of a group of Jews in the year 132 who fought the final struggle against Rome to try to preserve Jewish independence.

Michener, James. *The source.* **Random, 1965.**
A very long novel that spans 12,000 years. It tells the stories of fifteen different settlements that occupied the site of an ancient spring in Israel, as revealed by digging.

Mitchison, Naomi. *Blood of the martyrs.* **McGraw, 1948.**
Long novel about the persecution of the Christians during Nero's reign, and of the religious faith of the period.

Paul, Louis. *Dara, the Cypriot.* **Simon & Schuster, 1958.**
A wanderer's experiences in the Eastern Mediterranean lands in the 9th century B.C.

Schmitt, Gladys. *David the king.* **Dial, 1946.**
Long and unusually fine novel based on David's life, following
faithfully the Biblical accounts.

Shamir, Moshe. *David's stranger.* **Abelard, 1965.**
Story about Uriah the Hittite, Bath-Sheba's husband, whom David
sent into battle to be killed.

Slaughter, Frank G. *God's warrior.* **Doubleday, 1967.**
Good portrayal of the Jewish-Gentile differences in first-century
Palestine. Luke the Physician plays a role.

Slaughter, Frank G. *Scarlet cord.* **Doubleday, 1956.**
Based on the story of Rahab, the woman of Jericho described in the
Book of Joshua. Good re-creation of the 12th century B.C.

Slaughter, Frank G. *The sins of Herod.* **Doubleday, 1968.**
Story with a religious atmosphere, in which the Apostles James and
John figure prominently.

Slaughter, Frank G. *Song of Ruth.* **Doubleday, 1954.**
A rather melodramatic rendition of the Bible story.

Slaughter, Frank G. *Thorn of Arimathea.* **Doubleday, 1959.**
Biblical period novel, set partly in Judea and partly in druidic Britain.

Slaughter, Frank G. *Upon this rock.* **Coward, 1963.**
An excellent novel based upon the life of the Apostle Peter.

Southon, Arthur E. *On eagles' wings.* **McGraw, 1953.**
Good fictional account of Moses and the Hebrew exodus.

Tandrup, Harald. *Reluctant prophet.* **Knopf, 1939.**
Interesting and often humorous story of Jonah, depicted as a little
Tyrian cake-seller to whom came the call to go to Nineveh and
prophesy.

Waltari, Mika. *Secret of the kingdom.* Putnam, 1961.
Young Roman nobleman arrives in Jerusalem at the time of the Crucifixion, and sees the effects on the community.

Watkins, Shirley. *The prophet and the king.* Doubleday, 1956.
About the prophet Samuel in his old age, and the young king Saul.

Weinreb, Nathaniel. *The Babylonians.* Doubleday, 1953.
Cloak-and-dagger story set in the court of Nebuchadnezzar in ancient Babylon.

Weinreb, Nathaniel. *The sorceress.* Doubleday, 1954.
Full of action and conflict, this story centers around Deborah, the Hebrew prophetess.

Wibberley, Leonard. *The centurion.* Morrow, 1966.
Vivid novel of Jerusalem during the period of Christ's life, seen through the eyes of a Roman officer.

Williams, Jay. *Solomon and Sheba.* Random, 1959.
Well-written story about the reign of Solomon.

Wilson, Dorothy. *The gifts.* McGraw, 1957.
Story of Jesus' boyhood.

Wilson, Dorothy. *The herdsman.* Westminster, 1947.
Biblical story of the minor prophet, Amos, and his times and people.

JUVENILE

Benjamin, Nora. *King Solomon's horses.* Harper, 1956.
Good adventure story of an Israelite lad serving in Solomon's forces against the Egyptians.

Benjamin, Nora. *King Solomon's navy.* Harper, 1954.
Adventures of a Hebrew boy on a voyage down the African coast to find gold and to bring a gift from Solomon to the Queen of Sheba.

Bothwell, Jean. *Flame in the sky.* **Vanguard, 1954.**
A story of the times of the Prophet Elijah.

Daringer, Helen. *Golden thorn.* **Harcourt, 1956.**
Romantic story for girls set in Judea at the time of Christ.

Godwin, Stephani and Edward. *Roman eagles.* **Oxford U.P., 1951.**
Story of a young Roman soldier and a Jewish girl in the first century.

Hyman, Frieda. *Jubal and the prophet.* **Farrar, 1958.**
In the time of Nebuchadnezzar, a Jewish boy is a follower of Jeremiah the prophet, whom his father opposes.

King, Marian. *Young King David.* **Lippincott, 1948.**
A good fictional treatment of the early life of David until he became king.

Malvern, Gladys. *Behold your queen!* **Longmans, 1951.**
Romantic story for girls about Esther, the Hebrew girl who became queen of the Persians.

Malvern, Gladys. *Saul's daughter.* **Longmans, 1956.**
A story about the romance between David, the shepherd boy, and Michal, King Saul's daughter.

Malvern, Gladys. *Tamar.* **Longmans, 1952.**
A story for girls about Capernaum in Christ's time.

Speare, Elizabeth. *The bronze bow.* **Houghton, 1961.**
About a Jewish boy in the time of Christ who belongs to an underground group fighting Roman domination.

EUROPE

EUROPE BEFORE 1500

Adams, Doris S. *The price of blood.* **Scribner, 1966.**
Story of a Christian Dane in 9th century Devon, torn between his
faith and his warlike countrymen. Good setting and action.

Almedingen, Martha. *Golden sequence.* **Westminster, 1949.**
A story of medieval French peasant life, best for its richness of
description.

Andrew, Prudence. *The constant star.* **Putnam, 1964.**
Set in England at the time of the Peasants' Revolt of 1381, this is the
story of conflict between two men — one a staunch conservative and
one looking to a new future.

Andrew, Prudence. *The hooded falcon.* **New Authors Guild, 1961.**
Story of a young nobleman caught in the stress of divided loyalties
to Wales and England in the 15th century.

Andrew, Prudence. *Ordeal by silence.* **Putnam, 1961.**
A young deaf-mute at the court of English king Henry II gains a
reputation as a saint, and after his death efforts are made to have
the Church canonize him.

Andrew, Prudence. *A sparkle from the coal.* **Putnam, 1965.**
Story of a 14th century Oxford student who leaves to become a
hermit and to try to find some meaning in religion.

Andrzejewski, Jerzy. *The inquisitors.* **Knopf, 1960.**
About Torquemada and the Spanish Inquisition of the Middle Ages,
it is also a strong sermon against tyranny and terror at any time or
place.

Barnes, Margaret. *Isabel the fair.* **Macrae Smith, 1957.**
Story about Edward II's French queen.

21

Barnes, Margaret. *Passionate brood*. Macrae Smith, 1945.
Novel based on the life of Richard I of England.

Barnes, Margaret. *Tudor rose*. Macrae Smith, 1953.
Story about the life of Elizabeth of York, the mother of Henry VIII.

Barnes, Margaret. *Within the hollow crown*. Macrae Smith, 1947.
A novel about Richard II, highly sympathetic to him.

Bengtsson, Frans. *Long ships*. Knopf, 1954.
Long but very gripping and well-written novel of the Vikings around
the year 1000. The settings cover much of the various territories
the Norsemen raided in those days.

Bourne, Peter. *Courts of love*. Putnam, 1958.
Romance and the life of a troubadour in medieval France.

Bourne, Peter. *When God slept*. Putnam, 1956.
Action and adventure in a story about two 12th century Englishmen
captured by Arabs while on a Crusade.

Braider, Donald. *An epic joy*. Putnam, 1971.
A novel about Peter Paul Rubens, Dutch painter and diplomat.

Breslin, Howard. *The gallowglass*. Crowell, 1958.
Colorful story, full of interesting action, set in Ireland about a
thousand years ago, when petty kings made war on each other.

Brooke, Teresa. *Under the winter moon*. Doubleday, 1958.
Romantic novel in the setting of medieval France and the First
Crusade.

Bryher. *Fourteenth of October*. Pantheon, 1952.
Excellent novel of England in 1066. Besides vivid action, there is a
masterly picture of the 11th century scene.

Bryher. *Ruan.* Pantheon, 1960.
Excellent novel about a young man in 6th century Britain who prefers searching for new places to remaining at home in Cornwall to become a druid priest.

Bryher. *This January tale.* Harcourt, 1966.
Powerful picture of the effects of the Norman Conquest on the Saxon people.

Carleton, Patrick. *Under the Hog.* Dutton, 1938.
Exciting and colorful story of 15th century England, centering about Richard III.

Carton, Jacques. *La Belle Sorel.* Washburn, 1956.
Good novel about the beautiful mistress of Charles VII of medieval France.

Challis, George. *Golden knight.* Greystone, 1937.
Rousing adventure tale about Richard Coeur-de-Lion and his times.

Charques, Dorothy. *Men like shadows.* Coward, 1952.
Well-written novel about the Third Crusade, in which three friends follow King Richard to Palestine. Adventure and pageantry.

Charques, Dorothy. *The nunnery.* Coward, 1960.
Good account of the period when Henry VIII ordered the dissolution of the monasteries. Central in the story is a nunnery in Warwickshire.

Chidsey, Donald B. *This bright sword.* Crown, 1957.
Novel of adventure in which an English knight fights with the barons against the unpopular King John.

Closs, Hannah. *Deep are the valleys.* Vanguard, 1961.
Story of the Albigensian Crusade in 13th century France.

Closs, Hannah. *High are the mountains.* **Vanguard, 1959.**
Well-written novel of the Albigensian Crusade and the siege of Carcassonne.

Closs, Hannah. *The silent tarn.* **Vanguard, 1963.**
Third in a trilogy of fine novels dealing with the Albigensian revolts in the Middle Ages.

Colyton, Henry. *Sir Pagan.* **Creative Age, 1947.**
Colorful adventure in the First Crusade.

Costain, Thomas B. *Below the salt.* **Doubleday, 1957.**
Long but vividly colorful novel of England under King John.

Costain, Thomas B. *Darkness and the dawn.* **Doubleday, 1959.**
Richly-colored story of two lovers who were drawn up in the struggle of civilized people against the invasion of Attila the Hun.

Costain, Thomas B. *The moneyman.* **Doubleday, 1947.**
A colorful pageant of France in the 15th century, centering about Jacques Coeur, the king's financial genius, and the king's mistress, Agnes Sorel.

Creed, Will. *Sword of Il Grande.* **Little, 1948.**
Novel of action and swordplay in an Italian city-state in the 15th century.

Cronquist, Mabel. *Bianca.* **Putnam, 1956.**
Intrigue and violent activity among a flamboyant cast of characters in the Italian city states of the 1400's.

Davis, Christopher. *Belmarch.* **Viking, 1964.**
A novel about the massacre of Jews during the First Crusade, but allegorical and philosophical as well as full of action.

Davis, M. H. *The winter serpent.* **McGraw, 1958.**
Story of Viking raids in 9th century Scotland.

Deiss, Joseph. *Great infidel.* **Random, 1963.**
Long colorful biographical novel about one of the more interesting
and remarkable medieval figures, Federico II, King of Sicily.

Deutsch, Babette. *Rogue's legacy.* **Coward, 1942.**
A colorful novel about Francois Villon and the Paris he knew.

De Wohl, Louis. *Lay siege to heaven.* **Lippincott, 1960.**
Novel based on the life of Saint Catherine of Siena, the 14th century
nun who was one of the most remarkable of medieval women.

Druon, Maurice. *The Iron King.* **Scribner, 1956.**
About Philip IV (The Fair) of France in 1314 and the intricate plots
involving his three daughters-in-law, the Knights Templar, and the
Lombard bankers.

Druon, Maurice. *The lily and the lion.* **Scribner, 1961.**
The last of six novels dealing with the downfall of the Capetian line
in medieval France. This book includes the period of the English
victories at Crecy and Poitiers.

Druon, Maurice. *The poisoned crown.* **Scribner, 1957.**
One of a series of novels about the French kings in the medieval
period, this centers about Louis X and his marriage to the daughter
of Charles Martel. Historically authentic.

Druon, Maurice. *Royal succession.* **Scribner, 1958.**
Vivid novel about Philip V of France, one of the "accursed" line of
Capetian kings.

Druon, Maurice. *The she-wolf of France.* **Scribner, 1960.**
About Isabella, Edward II's queen, and her lover, Roger Mortimer.
The tragic and brutal events of Edward's reign are portrayed with
great realism.

Druon, Maurice. *The strangled queen.* **Scribner, 1957.**
In Druon's series about the medieval French monarchy, this deals
with the short reign of Louis the Self-Willed, in the early 14th
century.

Du Bois, Theodora. *The emerald crown.* **Funk, 1955.**
A story of 9th century Ireland, with vivid and well-researched settings.

Du Bois, Theodora. *Love of Fingin O'Lea.* **Appleton, 1957.**
Set in Ireland of the 12th century, this is the story of how a young man grows up to become a noted European physician.

Duggan, Alfred. *Conscience of the king.* **Coward, 1952.**
Good story of early pre-Norman Britain, well developed from the few facts known of that period.

Duggan, Alfred. *Count Bohemund.* **Pantheon, 1965.**
Story of the First Crusade, centering around the Norman nobleman whose efforts and leadership did much to make the expedition successful.

Duggan, Alfred. *Cunning of the dove.* **Pantheon, 1960.**
A quiet but good historical account in fiction form of the character and reign of Edward the Confessor, last Saxon king of England.

Duggan, Alfred. *Leopards and lilies.* **Coward, 1954.**
Good fictional description of England under King John. Both the history and the plot are well done.

Duggan, Alfred. *The little emperors.* **Coward, 1952.**
An amusing and interesting story about a Roman civil servant in 5th century Britain.

Duggan, Alfred. *Lord Geoffrey's fancy.* **Pantheon, 1962.**
Story of adventure and exciting events in the struggles between Byzantines and Franks in the late 1200's.

Duggan, Alfred. *My life for my sheep.* **Coward, 1955.**
Not quite a novel, but a fictionalized and interesting account of the epic struggle between Henry II and Thomas Becket to determine the king's power versus the church.

Duggan, Alfred. *The right line of Cerdic.* Pantheon, 1961.
Story of Alfred the Great's struggles to defend England against
the Northmen.

Duncan, David. *Trumpet of God.* Doubleday, 1956.
Well-written novel of the Children's Crusade.

Edmondston, C. M. and Hyde, M. L. F. *King's man.* Longmans, 1948.
Good historical romance and adventure novel, centering on William
of Newbury, faithful adherent of Henry II of England. Sound and
interesting picture of 12th and 13th century Britain.

Ellis, Kenneth. *Guns forever echo.* Messner, 1941.
A story set in Yarmouth, England, in the 14th century during the
Hundred Years War and the Black Death.

Fast, Howard. *Torquemada.* Doubleday, 1966.
Story about the Spanish Inquisition in the period of Ferdinand and
Isabella.

Faure, Raoul. *Lady Godiva and Master Tom.* Harper, 1948.
A highly original and interesting version of the Godiva legend, set
in a fascinating medieval background.

Fergusson, Adam. *Roman go home.* Putnam, 1969.
A satirical and amusing novel about Celtic revolutionaries in 5th
century Britain, where the Romans cannot understand the native
ingratitude for the blessings of civilization.

Feuchtwanger, Lion. *Raquel.* Messner, 1955.
Romantic novel of 12th century Spain under Alfonso VIII, and
involving the intertwined problems of Christians, Jews and Moslems.

Fisher, F. H. *Written in the stars.* Harper, 1951.
A well-told biographical description of the artist, Albrecht Durer,
and of Nuremberg in the late 1400's.

Frankland, Edward. *Foster brothers.* **Day, 1954.**
Full of sometimes brutal but always interesting action. Vikings in
11th century England.

Fremantle, Anne. *James and Joan.* **Holt, 1948.**
A novel of 15th century England and Scotland, featuring the romance
of James I of Scotland and Joan Beaufort, and the colorful intrigues
of the English court.

Gartner, Chloe. *The infidels.* **Doubleday, 1960.**
Adventures of a young knight in the First Crusade.

Gay, Laverne. *The unspeakables.* **Scribner, 1945.**
This is a richly-pictured story of Lombardy in the 6th century, and
of Gregory the Great. Background material is very colorful.

Gerson, Noel B. *The Conqueror's wife.* **Doubleday, 1957.**
Vivid picture of 11th century England and of William I and his
queen, Matilda.

Greene, Anne. *Lady in the mask.* **Harper, 1942.**
Romance and picaresque adventure in Renaissance Italy.

Greenberg, Joanne. *The King's persons.* **Holt, 1963.**
A novel about the Jews in 12th century England, tolerated only
because of their usefulness to the king. The story is set in York,
culminating in the massacre of 1190.

Harwood, Alice. *Merchant of the Ruby.* **Bobbs, 1950.**
Historical romance of Catherine Gordon, cousin to the Scottish king,
and Perkin Warbeck, pretender to the crown of England.

Haughton, Rosemary. *Elizabeth's greeting.* **Lippincott, 1968.**
Set in medieval Germany, this is a biographical novel of Elizabeth of
Hungary, who became a saint of the church as a result of her faith
and her efforts to improve the society she found herself in.

Haycraft, Molly C. *My lord brother the Lion Heart.* Lippincott, 1968.
Story of Richard I and his sister Joan, in the setting of the Crusades.
Colorful and especially appealing to women.

Hicks Beach, Susan. *Cardinal of the Medici.* Cambridge U.P., 1937.
Novel of the Renaissance, well-written and vivid in its authentic
setting.

Hill, Pamela. *Marjorie of Scotland.* Putnam, 1956.
Interesting picture of medieval Scotland in this novel about the
daughter of Robert the Bruce.

Holland, Cecelia. *Antichrist.* Atheneum, 1970.
A highly colorful novel about the 13th century Holy Roman Em-
peror, Frederick II, one of the most fascinating personalities of the
Middle Ages.

Holland, Cecelia. *The firedrake.* Atheneum, 1966.
Story of a professional soldier in Europe and finally in England
serving William the Conqueror.

Holland, Cecelia. *Kings in winter.* Atheneum, 1968.
Set in 11th century Ireland, it is a story of warring clans and Gaelic
violence.

Holland, Cecilia. *Until the sun falls.* Atheneum, 1968.
The setting is the Mongol invasion of Europe in the 13th century.
Much violence and colorful background.

Jackson, Dorothy. *Walk with peril.* Putnam, 1959.
Story of a young Welshman who goes to the court of Henry V in
London and becomes involved in intrigues and romance. He gains
the King's favor at the Battles of Harfleur and Agincourt.

Jefferis, Barbara. *Beloved lady.* Sloane, 1955.
Romance and family life in the complicated setting of 15th century
England and the Wars of the Roses. Good historical realism.

29

John, Evan. *Crippled splendour.* **Dutton, 1938.**
Good novel of 15th century England and Scotland, in which the central figure is James I of Scotland.

Kamban, Gudmundur. *I see a wondrous land.* **Putnam, 1938.**
Good novel based on those portions of the Icelandic sagas which describe Leif Ericson's voyages to Vinland.

Kazantzakis, Nikos. *Saint Francis.* **Simon & Schuster, 1962.**
A novel based on the life of Francis of Assisi, who sought "in what manner and by what kind of struggle the flesh becomes spirit."

Kesten, Hermann. *Ferdinand and Isabella.* **Wyn, 1946.**
Fictionalized biography, chiefly of Isabella, who is depicted as a good woman who did much harm to Spain through her strong but unwise policies.

Koningsberger, Hans. *A walk with love and death.* **Simon & Schuster, 1961.**
Well-told love story set against a background of medieval France rent by intrigue and violence.

Kossak-Szczucka, Zofja. *Blessed are the meek.* **Roy, 1944.**
A strong novel of the Children's Crusade, and of St. Francis of Assisi.

Lagerkvist, Par. *The dwarf.* **L. B. Fischer, 1945.**
An unusual novel. The narrator is an evil and bitter court dwarf to one of the nobles of the Italian Renaissance. His view of his times is the essence of the story.

Leary, Francis. *Fire and morning.* **Putnam, 1957.**
The Wars of the Roses and Richard III are the subjects of this novel. Richard is not the traditional villain he once was; that place is taken by Henry Tudor.

Leary, Francis. *The swan and the rose.* **Wyn, 1953.**
Exciting story of a young Englishman who, in 1471, is fighting in the Lancastrian cause in the Wars of the Roses.

Leslie, Doris. *Vagabond's way*. Doubleday, 1962.
Interesting fictional treatment of the career of Francois Villon.

Lewis, Hilda W. *Wife to Henry V*. Putnam, 1957.
About the French princess who became an English queen for two years, and about the color and pageantry of medieval England.

Lewis, Hilda. *Wife to the bastard*. McKay, 1967.
Novel based on the life of Matilda, wife of William the Conqueror.

Lofts, Norah. *Lute player*. Doubleday, 1951.
Psychological novel about Richard I and the minstrel Blondel.

Lofts, Norah. *Town house*. Doubleday, 1959.
A story of three generations of a family in medieval England. Excellent pictures of old English customs and settings.

Maass, Edgar. *Magnificent enemies*. Scribner, 1955.
A full-color picture of the great power and internal rivalries of the 15th century cities of the Hanseatic League. There are also several vivid romances.

Maiden, Cecil. *Harp into battle*. Crowell, 1959.
Set in 12th century Wales, it tells of high adventure in the company of Llewelyn the Great.

Mann, Thomas. *The holy sinner*. Knopf, 1951.
Beautifully written rendition of a medieval Christian legend.

Marshall, Edison. *Pagan king*. Doubleday, 1959.
Action-packed story based on the Arthurian legend, but with different characters.

Mason, Van Wyck. *Silver leopard*. Doubleday, 1955.
The setting is the First Crusade, and the story is replete with melodrama, color and fast action.

Masters, John. *The rock.* **Putnam, 1970.**
An ingenious fictional device provides a gripping picture of Gibraltar's important part in the history of twenty centuries.

Maughan, A. Margery. *Harry of Monmouth.* **Sloane, 1956.**
Long, colorful and gripping novel about Henry V of England and his times.

Muntz, Hope. *Golden warrior.* **Scribner, 1949.**
Exceptionally fine novel of 11th century England and the events and conditions that produced the Battle of Hastings.

Mydans, Shelley. *Thomas.* **Doubleday, 1965.**
Long, panoramic and colorful novel based on the life of Thomas Becket.

Myers, Henry. *Utmost island.* **Crown, 1951.**
A Viking story of Iceland and Leif Ericson around 975.

Nathan, Robert. *The fair.* **Knopf, 1964.**
The setting is Anglo-Saxon England, just after the Arthurian period. The characters are an old abbot and two children, and an assortment of whimsical others — a druidess, gypsies and so on. A pleasant story for young and old.

O'Grady, Rohan. *O'Houlihan's jest.* **Macmillan, 1961.**
Well-written tale of early Ireland, with drama, Irish wit, and the genuine spirit of Celtic adventure.

Oldenbourg, Zoe. *Cities of the flesh.* **Pantheon, 1963.**
Vivid portrayal of the intense religious warfare of the 12th and 13th centuries known as the Albigensian Crusade.

Oldenbourg, Zoe. *The cornerstone.* **Pantheon, 1955.**
A long book about the Crusades, sequel to *The world is not enough.* Medieval France is pictured in all its color and pageantry.

Oldenbourg, Zoe. *Destiny of fire.* **Pantheon, 1961.**
An impressive novel about the Albigensian Crusade of the early 13th century. Good medieval background.

Oldenbourg, Zoe. *The world is not enough.* **Pantheon, 1948.**
A novel of castle life and adventure in medieval France. It is overly long, but the historical picture is authentic and realistic.

Oliver, Jane. *The lion is come.* **Putnam, 1957.**
Fictionalized biography of Robert Bruce of 13th century Scotland.

Oliver, Jane. *Sing, morning star.* **Putnam, 1956.**
The story of Malcolm Canmore, the king of Scotland in the 11th century, and of his wife Margaret — a romance.

Palmer, Marian. *White boar.* **Doubleday, 1968.**
Excellent novel of the complex loyalties in late 15th century England, with Richard III, Henry Tudor, Warwick, Percy and other famous figures.

Pargeter, Edith. *Heaven tree.* **Doubleday, 1960.**
Colorful and vigorous story of early 13th century England; the building of a cathedral is the central theme.

Pei, Mario. *Swords of Anjou.* **Day, 1952.**
A well-written story of medieval Spain based on the Song of Roland and other knightly legends.

Pierce, Glenn. *Tyrant of Bagdad.* **Little, 1955.**
Melodrama of the adventures of a Frankish count at the court of Charlemagne, in Constantinople and in Bagdad. Good entertainment.

Plaidy, Jean. *Goldsmith's wife.* **Appleton, 1950.**
Story about Jane Shore, who became mistress to Edward IV of England.

Potter, Jeremy. *A trail of blood.* **McCall, 1970.**
A novel about the "true" solution of the murders of the Princes in the Tower.

Powers, Anne. *Ride east! Ride west!* **Bobbs, 1947.**
Story of the Hundred Years War, set in Ireland and England.

Prescott, Hilda. *Son of dust.* **Macmillan, 1956.**
This well-written tale of the struggle between sacred and profane love is set in 11th century Normandy.

Prescott, Hilda. *Unhurrying chase.* **Macmillan, 1955.**
Excellent story set in medieval France about a youth who has his lands confiscated, and becomes a wanderer with a talent for singing.

Prokosch, Frederic. *Tale for midnight.* **Little, 1955.**
Vivid and blood-curdling story about the murder of Francesco Cenci in 16th century Italy, and of events that followed.

Roberts, Dorothy. *Kinsmen of the Grail.* **Little, 1963.**
Well-written novel, set in Wales, about Sir Perceval and Sir Gawin and their search for the Holy Grail. Good re-working of the Arthurian legends.

Roberts, Dorothy. *Launcelot, my brother.* **Appleton, 1954.**
A well-told and original rendering of the King Arthur legends, purportedly by Bors de Ganis, Launcelot's brother.

Roberts, Dorothy. *Return of the stranger.* **Appleton, 1958.**
Story of ancient Ireland, based on the legend of Etain, the lost waif who became wife to the High King of Ireland.

Samuel, Maurice. *Web of Lucifer.* **Knopf, 1947.**
A good action novel of Renaissance Italy in the time of Cesare Borgia. Color and excitement.

Schofield, William. *The deer cry.* Longmans, 1948.
The life and works of St. Patrick told as an interesting novel.

Schoonover, Lawrence. *Burnished blade.* Macmillan, 1948.
Well-told adventure story of 15th century France, with many colorful episodes.

Schoonover, Lawrence. *Queen's cross.* Sloane, 1955.
Romanticized story of Isabella of Spain, consort of Ferdinand. Good picture of 15th century Spain.

Schoonover, Lawrence. *Spider king.* Macmillan, 1954.
Long and minutely detailed novel about 15th century France in the time of Louis XI.

Seton, Anya. *Avalon.* Houghton, 1966.
Set in Saxon England of the 10th century, with a realistic historical background, and involving the Arthurian legend and other myths.

Seton, Anya. *Katherine.* Houghton, 1953.
A long, vivid and well-told novel set in medieval England. The heroine is Katherine Swynford, Chaucer's sister-in-law and John of Gaunt's wife.

Shellabarger, Samuel. *Prince of foxes.* Little, 1947.
Romance and intrigue in Cesare Borgia's Italy, with good historical setting and realism.

Shellabarger, Samuel. *The token.* Little, 1955.
Romance of medieval France during the Crusades.

Shipway, George. *Imperial governor.* Doubleday, 1968.
Story of the struggle between the British Queen Boudicca and the Roman legions in the 1st century. Has both action and good background.

Shipway, George. *The knight.* Doubleday, 1970.
A well-written and vivid story of 12th century England, in which Geoffrey de Mandeville is a principal figure.

Shore, Maxine. *Captive princess.* Longmans, 1952.
Enjoyable story of pagan Britain in the first century, and also of early Christianity in Rome.

Simon, Edith. *Golden hand.* Putnam, 1952.
A novel of England in the time of Richard II. Its chief attraction lies in the realistic portrayal of 14th century life and customs.

Simon, Edith. *Twelve pictures.* Putnam, 1955.
A series of episodes comprising facets of the Niebelungenlied and other medieval myths, woven together into a colorful and picturesque tale.

Slaughter, Frank G. *The mapmaker.* Doubleday, 1957.
Sea-faring adventure in the late 15th century. Prince Henry of Portugal.

Spinatelli, Carl. *The Florentine.* Prentice, 1953.
Fictionalized biography of Benvenuto Cellini.

Steedman, Marguerite. *Refuge in Avalon.* Doubleday, 1961.
Story about Joseph of Arimathea, legendary grand-uncle of Jesus, who reportedly came to Britain after the Crucifixion.

Street, James. *Velvet doublet.* Doubleday, 1952.
An unusual and interesting picture of Spain and North Africa as Columbus saw it.

Tey, Josephine. *Daughter of time.* Macmillan, 1952.
An historical detective novel, extremely well done. An English police officer of today, laid up in a hospital, undertakes to determine by reading and reason, whether Richard III really had his nephews killed.

Treece, Henry. *Golden strangers.* **Random, 1956.**
An unusual and interesting novel that tries to picture Britain in the time when the Iron Age was slowly replacing the New Stone Age.

Treece, Henry. *Great captains.* **Random, 1955.**
An excellent effort to make real the last centuries of the Dark Ages in Britain, using the Arthurian legends and other Celtic traditions. Colorful and vivid.

Treece, Henry. *Red queen, white queen.* **Random, 1958.**
Story about Boadicea's struggle against Roman conquerors in 1st century Britain.

Walworth, Alice. *Shield of honor.* **Doubleday, 1957.**
Story of an English knight's adventures as a follower of Simon de Montfort, rebel against the king in medieval England.

Walworth, Alice. *Vows of the peacock.* **Doubleday, 1955.**
Excellent historical background in this novel about Edward II's queen, Isabel of France, and of Elizabeth of Warwick.

Warner, Sylvia. *The corner that held them.* **Viking, 1948.**
An engrossing picture of daily life in an English convent during the 14th century.

Weenolsen, Hebe. *The last Englishman.* **Doubleday, 1951.**
Vigorous and lively novel about Hereward the Wake's valiant efforts to maintain English independence from the Normans.

Wescott, Jan. *The White Rose.* **Putnam, 1969.**
Novel based on the love story of Edward IV and Elizabeth Woodville, which played an important part in the Wars of the Roses. The story covers the thirty years of conflict, murder and intrigue.

White, Helen C. *Bird of fire.* **Macmillan, 1958.**
Biographical novel about St. Francis of Assisi.

White, Helen C. *Not built with hands.* Macmillan, 1935.
Superior novel of 11th century Europe, in which Pope Gregory VII and Countess Matilda of Tuscany are chief figures. Portrays powerfully the medieval struggle between papal and secular power.

White, Olive B. *The king's good servant.* Macmillan, 1936.
Good fictional portrait of Sir Thomas More in the last tragic years of his life.

White, T. H. *The once and future king.* Putnam, 1958.
One of the classic versions of the Arthurian legends. Beautiful writing and enjoyable wit.

Whittle, Tyler. *Richard III: the last Plantagenet.* Chilton, 1970.
A novel about the career and court of one of England's most controversial monarchs.

Williams, Jay. *The siege.* Little, 1955.
Well-told story, with vivid settings, of the Albigensian Crusade in 13th century France.

Williams, Jay. *Tomorrow's fire.* Atheneum, 1964.
Story of the Third Crusade, as purportedly told from the journal of a wandering trouvère. Good action and colorful settings.

Woods, William. *Riot at Gravesend.* Little, 1952.
Romantic story with an exciting background in the Peasants' Revolt in England in 1381.

JUVENILE

Andrews, Frank. *For Charlemagne!* Harper, 1949.
Story of a boy who, in 789, comes to Charlemagne's court to study under Alcuin, and with other students foils a plot against the king.

Bailey, Ralph. *Argosies of empire.* Dutton, 1947.
Accounts of a number of pre-Columbus sailors who discovered the world's sea routes, told in fictional form.

Baumann, Hans. *Barque of the brothers.* **Walck, 1958.**
A story of two brothers involved in the activities of Prince Henry the Navigator.

Beaty, John. *Swords in the dawn.* **Longmans, 1937.**
About Hengist and Horsa, and life in early Britain.

Beers, Lorna. *Book of Hugh Flower.* **Harper, 1952.**
Story about a young mason in medieval England. Excellent background.

Behn, Harry. *Faraway lurs.* **World, 1963.**
A romantic story of the early Bronze Age of Europe, told in a semi-poetic prose.

Berry, Erick. *King's jewel.* **Viking, 1957.**
Exciting adventure story of King Alfred's fight against invading Danes.

Best, Herbert. *Sea warriors.* **Macmillan, 1959.**
An exciting well-written story of two Viking boys on a dangerous quest that takes them to Iceland, Greenland and Vinland.

Bolton, Ivy. *Son of the land.* **Messner, 1946.**
Story of a young English serf who takes his master's side in Wat Tyler's Rebellion.

Bowers, Gwendolyn. *Brother to Galahad.* **Walck, 1963.**
About a boy who goes to Camelot, is befriended by Galahad and takes part in some of the events that make up the Arthurian epic.

Bowers, Gwendolyn. *Lost dragon of Wessex.* **Walck, 1957.**
Story of a boy who serves King Alfred in the wars against the Danes.

Church, Richard. *Bells of Rye.* **Day, 1961.**

With fine writing but an intricate plot, this is a worthwhile story of Anglo-Norman warfare on the southern coast of England in 1377.

Coe, Frederick. *Knight of the cross.* **Sloane, 1951.**

Good story of the adventures of a Viking boy who sails all the way from Norway to Jerusalem in the First Crusade.

Corbett, Mary. *Girl of Urbino.* **Abelard, 1953.**

Story for girls set in the Italian Renaissance.

Dehkes, Evelyn. *The young Viking warrior.* **Bobbs, 1953.**

Story of adventure about a 12-year old Norwegian boy in the 9th century.

Del Rey, Lester. *Cave of spears.* **Knopf, 1957.**

Prehistoric cavemen of Europe and how they lived.

Evernden, Margery. *Knight of Florence.* **Random, 1950.**

Story of 14th century Florence in which the son of a noble family succeeds in becoming an artist instead of a soldier as he was supposed to be.

Faulkner, Nancy. *Sacred jewel.* **Doubleday, 1961.**

Adventure and excitement in druidical Britain, involving a young bard, a druid's daughter and a stolen gem.

Faulkner, Nancy. *The yellow hat.* **Doubleday. 1958.**

Story of a boy in London in 1381, who numbers Wat Tyler and Chaucer among his friends.

Harnett, Cynthia. *Caxton's challenge.* **World, 1960.**

Set in London in the late 15th century, this excellent story tells of the opposition to the printing press by the scribes of the city.

Harnett, Cynthia. *The drawbridge gate.* **Putnam, 1954.**

Story of three English children who become involved in Oldcastle's plot against Henry V.

Harnett, Cynthia. *Nicholas and the woolpack.* **Putnam, 1953.**
About a boy in 15th century England whose father is a wool merchant. Besides a good story, there is much information about the medieval wool trade.

Haugaard, Erik. *Hakon of Rogen's saga.* **Houghton, 1963.**
Realistic picture of a Viking community.

Haugaard, Erik. *A slave's tale.* **Houghton, 1965.**
Sequel to *Hakon of Rogen's Saga.*

Hodges, C. Walter. *The namesake.* **Coward, 1964.**
Novel based on the career and character of Alfred the Great.

Jewett, Eleanore. *Big John's secret.* **Viking, 1962.**
Story of an English boy's adventures in France in the 13th century.

Kent, Louise. *He went with Marco Polo.* **Houghton, 1935.**
Good adventure story of the experiences of a Venetian boy.

Ketchum, Philip. *The great axe Bretwalda.* **Little, 1955.**
Exciting adventures of a Briton in the 9th century who is twice captured by the Danes and twice escapes.

Knight, Ruth A. *Land beyond.* **McGraw, 1954.**
Vivid picture of the tragic Children's Crusade.

Knox, Esther. *Swift flies the falcon.* **Winston, 1939.**
Two young people of a noble English family travel across Europe to Antioch during the First Crusade.

Leighton, Margaret. *Judith of France.* **Houghton, 1948.**
Romantic historical novel about the granddaughter of Charlemagne.

Leighton, Margaret. *Voyage to Coromandel.* **Farrar, 1965.**
Two Viking hostages at court of Alfred the Great take part in a mission to Rome and India.

Lewis, Hilda. *Gentle falcon.* **Criterion, 1957.**
Good biographical novel about Isabella of France, the young girl who became Queen to England's Richard II.

Lewis, Hilda. *Here comes Harry.* **Criterion, 1960.**
Exciting story of events at the court of Henry VI in 15th century England.

Lofts, Norah. *Eleanor the queen.* **Doubleday, 1955.**
Excellent novel about Eleanor of Aquitaine, wife of England's Henry II.

Meyler, Eileen. *Gloriet tower.* **Roy, 1957.**
Story for girls about royal intrigues in 14th century England.

Meyler, Eileen. *Story of Elswyth.* **Roy, 1959.**
A story of a girl in 10th century England. A little romance, with adventure and fine historical background.

Oliver, Jane. *Young man with a sword.* **St. Martins, 1955.**
Story of a youth serving with Robert the Bruce at the 14th century Battle of Bannockburn.

Parker, R. *Sword of Ganelon.* **McKay, 1958.**
Exciting adventure in ninth-century Britain, with interesting background on medical ideas of the time.

Peart, Hendry. *Red falcons of Tremoine.* **Knopf, 1956.**
Colorful adventure story in medieval England, in which a boy is kidnaped by a wicked uncle but ultimately succeeds to his estate.

Picard, Barbara. *Lost John.* **Criterion, 1963.**
Good story of a boy who was captured by a band of outlaws which he
then joined. The setting is the Forest of Arden in the reign of
Richard I.

Picard, Barbara. *One is one.* **Holt, 1966.**
Good story of a medieval boy who, having been placed in a monastery
because he is artistic rather than strong, runs away to prove he is
worthy to become a knight.

Picard, Barbara. *Ransom for a knight.* **Walck, 1961.**
Well-written and vivid story of a girl's efforts to ransom her father
and brother, taken captive at Bannockburn in 1314.

Polland, Madeleine. *Beorn the proud.* **Holt, 1962.**
A Viking story for girls about an Irish girl captured in a raid on
Ireland and taken back to Denmark.

Polland, Madeleine. *Children of the red king.* **Holt, 1961.**
Set in England and Ireland at the time of the Norman Conquest.
Good background.

Polland, Madeleine. *Flame over Tara.* **Doubleday, 1964.**
Tale of adventure involving St. Patrick's mission to Ireland.

Polland, Madeleine. *Queen's blessing.* **Holt, 1964.**
A story of 11th century Scotland, in which Queen Margaret befriends two young Danish captives.

Powers, Anne. *Ride with danger.* **Bobbs, 1958.**
Story of a young Irish spy at the English court about 1340. Battle
of Crècy.

Ritchie, Rita. *Ice falcon.* **Norton, 1963.**
A Saxon boy makes a journey to Viking Iceland.

43

Rush, Philip. *Castle and the harp.* **McGraw, 1964.**
Realistic pictures of life in 13th century England.

Sandoz, Edouard. *Squire of Ravensmark.* **Houghton, 1949.**
Romantic adventures of a boy and girl held captive in a castle in 13th century England.

Schmeltzer, Kurt. *Axe of bronze.* **Sterling, 1958.**
Set in Britain in the Late Stone Age, and depicting the conflict between the old people and the new who used bronze tools.

Seredy, Kate. *White stag.* **Viking, 1937.**
Fine, beautifully illustrated book about the legendary founding of Hungary.

Sobol, Donald. *Double quest.* **Watts, 1957.**
Historical and mystery story with plenty of action. The setting is the 12th century England of chivalry and adventure.

Sprague, Rosemary. *Heir of Kiloran.* **Walck, 1956.**
Romance and excitement occur when two young Scottish noblemen come to Renaissance Florence.

Sprague, Rosemary. *Heroes of a white shield.* **Oxford U.P., 1955.**
Adventure story set in 11th century Norway.

Stephens, Peter. *Outlaw king.* **Atheneum, 1964.**
Exciting story of how Robert the Bruce fought for Scottish freedom.

Sutcliff, Rosemary. *Dawn wind.* **Walck, 1962.**
Story of a British lad who works as a thrall to a Saxon family in early England.

Sutcliff, Rosemary. *Knight's fee.* **Walck, 1960.**
Good story of feudal conditions and adventure in 11th century England.

Sutcliff, Rosemary. *Lantern bearers.* **Walck, 1959.**
Story of a Roman youth who remained in Britain after his troop left. He aids the British in their hopeless fight against invading Saxons.

Sutcliff, Rosemary. *Warrior scarlet.* **Walck, 1958.**
Set in Bronze Age Britain, this is a good story of a crippled boy's successful struggle to prove himself a warrior.

Trease, Geoffrey. *Escape to King Alfred.* **Vanguard, 1958.**
How an English boy and girl escape from the Danes and, through many adventures, reach King Alfred with an important warning.

Trease, Geoffrey. *Shadow of the Hawk.* **Harcourt, 1949.**
Exciting tale of the Renaissance, when a boy and girl encounter many trials while searching for a lost and valuable Greek manuscript.

Treece, Henry. *The burning of Njal.* **Criterion, 1964.**
Conflict and blood feuds in 11th century Iceland. Viking ways and legends well introduced.

Treece, Henry. *The horned helmet.* **Criterion, 1963.**
Dramatic story of an 11th century Viking voyage.

Treece, Henry. *The last Viking.* **Pantheon, 1966.**
Excellent portrayal of Harald, the Norseman who sought the throne of England in the 11th century.

Treece, Henry. *Man with a sword.* **Pantheon, 1964.**
Set in 11th century England, before and during the Norman Conquest. Interesting to adults as well as teen-agers.

Treece, Henry. *Men of the hills.* **Criterion, 1958.**
A boys' story about warfare, hunting and the often brutal life of neolithic Britain.

Treece, Henry. *Perilous pilgrimage.* **Criterion, 1959.**
Adventure and troubles in the Children's Crusade.

Treece, Henry. *Ride into danger.* **Criterion, 1959.**
Young Englishman in the reign of Edward III fights to protect his estate from invading Welsh. He also goes to France and fights at Crecy. Good medieval story.

Treece, Henry. *Road to Miklagard.* **Criterion, 1957.**
Sequel to *Viking's Dawn,* in which the young hero makes a journey to Constantinople.

Treece, Henry. *Splintered sword.* **Duell, 1966.**
Authentic picture of youthful adventure among the Vikings in Scotland about the 10th century. Vivid illustrations.

Treece, Henry. *Viking's dawn.* **Criterion, 1956.**
Story of a disastrous Viking raid on Britain, from which only one survivor returned home.

Treece, Henry. *Viking's sunset.* **Criterion, 1961.**
Third of a trilogy of stories, this puts the hero in his later years in America.

Treece, Henry. *Westward to Vinland.* **S. G. Phillips, 1967.**
Story based on the exploits of Eric the Red and his son, Leif Ericson.

Trevino, Elizabeth. *Casilda of the rising moon.* **Farrar, 1967.**
Romantic and mystical story of the daughter of a Moorish king in 11th century Toledo.

Vance, Marguerite. *Song for a lute.* **Dutton, 1958.**
Richard III and his queen are the central figures in this novel about the Wars of the Roses.

Welch, Ronald. *Bowman of Crecy.* **Criterion, 1967.**
Young Englishman trains a band of outlaws to be good archers and leads them in battle of Crecy.

Willard, Barbara. *If all the swords in England.* **Doubleday, 1961.**
Deals with the struggle for dominance between King Henry II and Archbishop Thomas Becket.

Williams, Jay. *Tournament of the lions.* **Walck, 1960.**
Two lads in medieval France learn the arts and traditions of chivalry, and the story of Roland and Oliver.

Williams, Ursula. *The earl's falconer.* **Morrow, 1961.**
Story set in medieval England and concerned mainly with the sport of falconry.

Yonge, Charlotte. *The little duke.* **Dutton, 1963.**
This story was first published in 1854. It is a story, in Victorian terms, of the boyhood of Richard the Fearless, third Duke of Normandy, in the 10th century.

EUROPE, 1500-1789

Andrew, Prudence. *A new creature.* **Putnam, 1968.**
Set in Bristol, England, in 1739, it tells of a brutal industrialist and slave-trader who was converted to a new life by the preaching of John Wesley, and found himself ostracized by his old associates.

Anthony, Evelyn. *Anne Boleyn.* **Crowell, 1957.**
The story of Henry VIII's ill-fated second queen.

Anthony, Evelyn. *Royal intrigue.* **Crowell, 1954.**
Realistic picture of Catherine the Great and her son Paul.

Barker, Shirley. *Liza Bowe.* **Random, 1956.**
Romantic and colorful tale of a young barmaid in the Mermaid Tavern in 1588.

47

Barnes, Margaret. *Brief gaudy hour*. Macrae Smith, 1949.
The story of Anne Boleyn and her love for Harry Percy.

Barnes, Margaret. *King's fool*. Macrae Smith, 1959.
About a youth who became court jester to Henry VIII and lived among the exciting events of the period.

Barnes, Margaret. *Mary of Carisbrooke*. Macrae Smith, 1955.
Romance and action in a story about the loyal girl who served Charles I in his imprisonment on the Isle of Wight.

Barnes, Margaret. *My lady of Cleves*. Macrae Smith, 1946.
Novel about Henry VIII's fourth wife, one of the best of the group, and about the intricate court life of the time.

Barton, Florence. *The sage and the olive*. Muhlenberg, 1953.
Story of an early 16th century Parisian printer who becomes involved in the beginnings of the French Reformation.

Beatty, John and Patricia. *Campion Towers*. Macmillan, 1965.
Set in the time of the English Civil War, of Cromwell and the Puritans, this story gives an excellent picture of the deep religious differences.

Bentley, Phyllis. *Power and the glory*. Macmillan, 1940.
Novel about two families of cousins in Yorkshire, one Puritan and one royalist, during the perid of the Civil War and Cromwell's rule.

Beresford-Howe, Constance. *My Lady Greensleeves*. Ballantine, 1954.
Story of an unsuccessful mixed-class marriage in the days of Elizabethan England.

Brady, Charles. *Stage of fools*. Dutton, 1952.
Serious and interesting novel portraying the rather tragic career of a great man, Sir Thomas More.

Bryher. *Player's boy.* **Pantheon, 1953.**
Good novel depicting England in the early 1600's following the Elizabethan period.

Buchan, John. *Blanket of the dark.* **Houghton, 1931.**
Story told by a master story-teller of an unsuccessful attempt to overthrow Henry VIII.

Buckmaster, Henrietta. *All the living.* **Random, 1962.**
A fictional picture of the year 1600 in Shakespeare's life; good descriptive portrait of a colorful scene.

Burgess, Anthony. *Nothing like the sun.* **Norton, 1964.**
This purports to be a story of young Shakespeare's love-life and urges, especially as he revealed them in his sonnets.

Byrd, Elizabeth. *Immortal queen.* **Ballentine, 1956.**
Good novel based on the life of Mary, Queen of Scots.

Campbell, Grace. *Torbeg.* **Little, 1952.**
A story of Scotland in the Jacobite uprising of 1745, especially interesting for its picture of the clans and old Scottish ways of life.

Caute, David. *Comrade Jacob.* **Pantheon, 1962.**
A novel of Cromwell's times, about a sect known as Diggers, searching for civil equality.

Chapman, Hester W. *Lucy.* **Reynal, 1966.**
Story of a girl who becomes an actress in the English Restoration theatre. Describes the society and life of the later Stuart period.

Charques, Dorothy. *Dark stranger.* **Coward, 1956.**
Intrigue and excitement, with good historical realism, in the struggle between Royalists and Puritans.

Chidsey, Donald B. *The legion of the lost.* **Crown, 1967.**
High adventure on board Captain Kidd's ship on the voyage in which he turns to piracy in the 1690's.

Christensen, Synnove. *Lindeman's daughters.* **Doubleday, 1958.**
Well-written picture of life in 18th century Norway.

Clark, Justus. *King's agent.* **Scribner, 1958.**
Story of the exile of James II and the many intrigues involving him.

Coryn, Marjorie. *Sorrow by day.* **Appleton, 1950.**
Vivid novel of French court life in the age of Louis XIV and his cousin La Grande Mademoiselle.

Crisp, Frank. *Golden quest.* **Coward, 1953.**
A tale of exciting adventure in the late 17th century ranging from Newgate Jail in London, pirates on the high seas, to the South Pacific.

Davidson, Diane. *Feversham.* **Crown, 1969.**
Exciting fictional account of a noted true murder case in Tudor England. A thriller in the real-life setting of the period.

Delves-Broughton, Josephine. *Heart of a queen.* **McGraw, 1950.**
Well-written novel portraying Elizabeth I of England as she probably really was.

De Wohl, Louis. *The last crusader.* **Lippincott, 1956.**
Novel centering on Don Juan of Austria, who defeated the Moors in Spain, and the Battle of Lepanto.

Dexter, Charles. *Street of kings.* **Holt, 1957.**
Melodrama in early 17th century England, centering about the mysterious murder of the poet, Sir Thomas Overbury.

Doncher, Anton. *Time of parting.* Morrow, 1968.
A Bulgarian author writes a powerful novel of the forcible conversion of a 17th century province to Islam under Turkish power.

Du Maurier, Daphne. *King's general.* Doubleday, 1946.
Colorful melodrama of Sir Richard Grenville and Cornwall in the middle 17th century.

Dunnett, Dorothy. *Game of kings.* Putnam, 1961.
Engrossing story of adventure and intrigue in 16th century Scotland.

Durbin, Charles. *The mercenary.* Houghton, 1963.
Renaissance Italy in 1520 and the adventures of a condottiere. Much fighting and bloodshed.

Eckerson, Olive. *My Lord Essex.* Holt, 1955.
An unusually good novel based on the relationship between Elizabeth I and Essex.

Endore, Guy. *Voltaire! Voltaire!* Simon & Schuster, 1961.
Portraits in fiction of Voltaire and Rousseau.

Fisher, Edward. *Best house in Stratford.* Abelard, 1965.
Third in a trilogy of stories based in Shakespeare's life and times. This portrays him as producer and actor.

Fisher, Edward. *Shakespeare and Son.* Abelard, 1962.
Enjoyable picture of the relationship between John Shakespeare of Stratford and his young son William, who had odd interests about play-acting.

Foote, Dorothy. *Constant star.* Scribner, 1959.
Colorful tale of the Tudor period centering around the glamorous figure of Francis Walsingham.

Ford, Ford Madox. *The fifth queen.* **Vanguard, 1963.**
A story around the life of Katherine Howard, Henry VIII's fifth wife. The historical background is excellent; the style impressionistic.

Frischauer, Paul. *Shepherd's crook.* **Scribner, 1951.**
Good melodrama and romance about a Huguenot girl in the France of Louis XIV.

Garfield, Leon. *Black Jack.* **Pantheon, 1969.**
Adventure, violence and romance in 18th century England. Good background and characterization.

Gerson, Noel. *The anthem.* **Lippincott, 1967.**
A good novel with a broad sweep about the de Montauban family and the religious struggles in France over several centuries, beginning with Henri IV in 1593.

Gerson, Noel. *Queen's husband.* **McGraw, 1960.**
About William of Orange who married Mary, the daughter of James II, and became joint ruler of England in 1688.

Gerson, Noel. *The scimitar.* **Farrar, 1955.**
Melodrama and adventure for an 18th century Englishman involved in the fighting against the Turks in the Balkans.

Golon, Anne and Serge. *Angélique.* **Lippincott, 1958.**
Colorful picture of high and low life, and adventure of all sorts, in Paris of Louis XIV.

Golon, Anne and Serge. *Angélique and the king.* **Lippincott, 1960.**
Vigorous and colorful story of high and low life at the court of Louis XIV in the 1670's.

Goudge, Elizabeth. *Towers in the mist.* **Coward, 1938.**
A quiet enjoyable novel of Oxford in Elizabethan times.

Goudge, Elizabeth. *White witch.* **Coward, 1957.**
Good portrayal of the Royalist and Puritan struggles in England in the reign of Charles I.

Graham, Winston. *The grove of eagles.* **Doubleday, 1964.**
Story about the son of the Governor of a Cornish castle in the last decade of the 1500's. Excellent period and local color.

Green, Anne. *Silent duchess.* **Harper, 1939.**
Told in the form of a memoir, the life of an imaginary French noble-woman in the years before the Reign of Terror, and during it.

Grierson, Edward. *Dark torrent of Glencoe.* **Doubleday, 1960.**
Story of the Campbell-MacDonald clan feud which reached a bloody climax at Glencoe in 1692.

Guinagh, Kevin. *Search for glory.* **Longmans, 1946.**
Story of French life in the 17th century, with vivid pictures of country estates, the cities, new discoveries in science, and so on. Good for school libraries.

Harsany, Zsolt. *The star-gazer.* **Putnam, 1939.**
Unusually fine novel dealing with the life of Galileo.

Harwood, Alice. *The lily and the leopards.* **Bobbs, 1949.**
Long but interesting novel about the tragic brief career of Lady Jane Grey.

Harwood, Alice. *Seats of the mighty.* **Bobbs, 1956.**
Authentic historical background in this novel about the Earl of Moray, half-brother to Mary, Queen of Scots.

Harwood, Alice. *So merciful a queen, so cruel a woman.* **Bobbs, 1958.**
Story of Elizabeth I and the two sisters of Lady Jane Grey. Intrigue and tragedy.

Haycraft, Molly C. *The reluctant queen*. **Lippincott, 1962.**
Romance about Mary Tudor, the younger sister of Henry VIII, who was married unwillingly to Louis XII of France, but on his early death returned to her real love, the Duke of Suffolk. The same basic story as the old favorite, "When Knighthood was in Flower."

Heyer, Georgette. *Royal escape*. **Doubleday, 1939.**
A story of the English Civil War and of Charles II's escape to France after the Battle of Worcester.

Hill, Pamela. *Crown and the shadow*. **Putnam, 1955.**
Fictional biography of Madame de Maintenon, the mistress of Louis XIV.

Holland, Cecelia. *Rakossy*. *Atheneum,* **1967.**
Story of a 16th century Hungarian patriot fighting Turkish inroads. Action and romance.

Holt, Victoria. *The Queen's confession*. **Doubleday, 1968.**
A fictionalized life of Marie Antoinette.

Houston, June. *Faith and the flame*. **Sloane, 1958.**
Romance and adventure in the setting of the religious wars in France at the time of Catherine de Medici.

Irwin, Margaret. *Elizabeth and the Prince of Spain*. **Harcourt, 1953.**
One of this author's novels about the life of Elizabeth I, this deals with the reign of her sister Mary.

Irwin, Margaret. *Gay galliard*. **Harcourt, 1942.**
The love story of Mary, Queen of Scots, and the Earl of Bothwell.

Irwin, Margaret. *Stranger prince*. **Harcourt, 1937.**
Good novel of the English Civil War, and especially of that romantic figure, Prince Rupert.

Jahoda, Gloria. *Annie.* Houghton, 1960.
Romantic story set in Norfolk, England, in the 17th century.

Jennings, John. *Wind in his fists.* Holt, 1955.
Tale of swashbuckling action between E·iropeans and Turks in the
Mediterranean in the mid-1500's.

Kenyon, Frank. *Mary of Scotland.* Crowell, 1957.
Biographical novel based on the life of Mary, Queen of Scots.

Kenyon, Frank. *Shadow in the sun.* Crowell, 1958.
Biographical novel about Elizabeth I of England.

Knight, Brigid. *Valiant lady.* Doubleday, 1948.
Story of a courageous Dutch woman who protects her family during
Holland's war of independence against Spain.

Lane, Jane. *Madame Geneva.* Rinehart, 1946.
Set in London in the early 1700's, this deals with a Jacobite plot and
the terrible condition of the poor at that period.

Lane, Jane. *Parcel of rogues.* Rinehart, 1948.
A long and engrossing novel about Mary, Queen of Scots, and the
dubious characters who surrounded her.

Letton, Jennette and Francis. *Robsart affair.* Harper, 1956.
Romantic novel based on the story of Elizabeth I's love for Robert
Dudley, whose wife, Amy Robsart, died mysteriously.

Letton, Jennette and Francis. *Young Elizabeth.* Harper, 1953.
A story of Elizabeth I in the years before she became queen.

Levy, Barbara. *Adrienne.* Holt, 1960.
Story based on the life of Adrienne Lecouvreur, actress and friend of
Voltaire in 18th century France.

Lewis, Ada. *Longest night.* **Rinehart, 1958.**
Lively and colorful adventure story against the background of the
St. Bartholomew's Day massacre in 16th century France.

Lewis, Hilda. *Call Lady Purbeck.* **St. Martins, 1962.**
Fictional treatment of a 17th century English scandal.

Lewis, Janet. *Ghost of Monsieur Scarron.* **Doubleday, 1959.**
Well-written and realistic novel, based on a true incident in the
reign of Louis XIV. Authentic background, good characterizations.

Linington, Elizabeth. *The kingbreaker.* **Doubleday, 1958.**
Story of a Welsh Royalist in the English Civil War who becomes a
spy in Cromwell's household.

Linington, Elizabeth. *Monsieur Janvier.* **Doubleday, 1957.**
Melodrama of the 18th century, set in Scotland, Paris and London.
Many famous people involved.

Linington, Elizabeth. *The proud man.* **Viking, 1955.**
Novel based on the career of Shane O'Neill, the Ulster chieftain who
in the 16th century almost brought about a free and united Ireland.

Lofts, Norah. *Colin Lowrie.* **Knopf, 1938.**
Adventures of a Scotsman forced to leave home after the 1745 uprising. His subsequent career takes him to the West Indies, to Virginia and finally home again.

Lofts, Norah. *The concubine.* **Doubleday, 1963.**
Vivid and well-written novel about Anne Boleyn and the court of
Henry VIII.

Lofts, Norah. *House at Old Vine.* **Doubleday, 1961.**
The individual stories of six persons who, at different times in the
16th and 17th centuries, lived in the house. Especially good for the
realism of the English setting.

MacInnes, Colin. *Three years to play.* **Farrar, 1970.**
Very enjoyable picaresque novel of Elizabethan England, in which Aubrey, a country boy, comes to London to seek his fortune and becomes a friend and associate of Shakespeare.

Macken, Walter. *Seek the fair land.* **Macmillan, 1959.**
Gripping tale about a young Irish merchant's struggle to survive the brutal invasion of Ireland by Cromwell's armies.

MacLeod, Alison. *City of light.* **Houghton, 1969.**
Third in a series of novels about Tom Vaughan, an English exile from the land of Queen Mary Tudor, this tale takes him into adventures in Geneva.

MacLeod, Alison. *The heretic.* **Houghton, 1966.**
Story of religious cruelty and a woman's persecution in the England of Henry VIII.

MacLeod, Alison. *The hireling.* **Houghton, 1968.**
Costume melodrama in the time of Henry VIII, involving many of the famous names of the period.

Mallet-Joris, Francoise. *The witches.* **Farrar, 1969.**
Three young Frenchwomen are the protagonists of the three stories in this book. All lived in the 16th century and all were condemned as witches. There are vivid accounts, in fiction form, of actual victims of the belief in demonology.

Mann, Heinrich. *Young Henry of Navarre.* **Knopf, 1937.**
Excellent novel about Henry before he became Henry IV of France.

Marshall, Edison. *The upstart.* **Farrar, 1945.**
Picaresque novel of adventure in the London slums and provincial theatres of 18th century England.

Mason, A. E. W. *Fire over England.* **Doubleday, 1936.**
Good novel of adventure and intrigue in England when the Armada threatened.

Mason, Van Wyck. *Golden admiral.* **Doubleday, 1952.**
Colorful and violent action in a glamorous setting. Novel about Drake and the Armada.

Mather, Berkely. *The road and the star.* **Scribner, 1965.**
Tale of swashbuckling adventure in the 17th century, ranging from London to South Africa and India. Pirates, shipwrecks, and many other bits of wild action.

Matthew, Anne. *Warm wind, west wind.* **Crown, 1956.**
Good descriptive material about the latter years of Henry VII, especially of the shipping industry and the life of the cities.

McKemy, Kay. *Samuel Pepys of the navy.* **Warne, 1970.**
A novel, in which Pepys is the narrator, which pictures England under the Puritans and during the restoration of Charles II. Colorful and interesting.

Morley, Iris. *We stood for freedom.* **Morrow, 1942.**
A romance of 17th century England and Monmouth's Rebellion, with vivid descriptions of conditions then.

Mujica-Lainez, Manuel. *Bomarzo.* **Simon & Schuster, 1969.**
Long, richly-colorful novel of the Renaissance in 15th century Italy, with intrigue and derring-do in abundance.

Murray, David. *Commander of the mists.* **Knopf, 1938.**
Good novel about the Scots rising of 1745 in support of Charles Stuart, the "Young Pretender."

Neill, Robert. *Black William.* **Doubleday, 1955.**
A pleasant story about Jacobite intrigue in 18th century Northumberland.

Neill, Robert. *Elegant witch.* **Doubleday, 1952.**
Vivid picture of 17th century England, especially of its belief in witchcraft.

Neill, Robert. *Hangman's cliff.* **Doubleday, 1956.**
Mystery and murder in this melodrama set on the east coast of England during the American Revolution.

Neill, Robert. *Rebel heiress.* **Doubleday, 1954.**
Melodrama and romance in this novel picturing the re-adjustments that had to occur with the restoration of Charles II after the Cromwellian interlude.

Neill, Robert. *Traitor's moon.* **Doubleday, 1952.**
Many interesting historical touches in this story of England in 1679, at the period of Titus Oates and the Popish Plot.

Nisser, Peter. *Red marten.* **Knopf, 1957.**
Stark and real picture of peasant life in eastern Sweden around 1700.

Oliver, Jane. *Flame of fire.* **Putnam, 1961.**
Well-written novel about the life of William Tyndale, the 16th century translator of the Bible. Good picture of the times and of the intense religious controversies.

Oliver, Jane. *Lion and the rose.* **Putnam, 1959.**
A sympathetic novel about Mary, Queen of Scots, her love affair with Bothwell and the murder of Darnley. A new interpretation of old mysteries.

O'Neill, Egan. *The Anglophile.* **Messner, 1957.**
A novel of intrigue and romance in 18th century Ireland, racked by Anglo-Irish violence.

Patrick, Joseph. *King's arrow.* **Lippincott, 1951.**
Adventure and excitement in the mid-1700's, involving smuggling and ranging from Scotland to the West Indies to Boston.

Payne, Robert. *Caravaggio.* **Little, 1968.**
Novel based on the life of this 16th century Italian artist.

Payne, Robert. *The roaring boys.* **Doubleday, 1955.**
Novel about Shakespeare and his fellow actors, stronger in vivid pictures of the times than in plot.

Pick, John B. *Last valley.* **Little, 1960.**
Story of a wandering band of mercenary soldiers in the Thirty Years War.

Pilgrim, David. *Grand design.* **Harper, 1943.**
Sequel to *No Common Glory,* this continues the adventures of James de la Cloche, son of Charles II.

Pilgrim, David. *No common glory.* **Harper, 1942.**
A novel of the adventures of a reputed son of Charles II, who plays a part in the tangled politics of the time.

Plaidy, Jean. *Madame Serpent.* **Appleton, 1951.**
Set in the 16th century, this is a colorful novel about Catherine de Medici, who is one of the more sinister figures in French history.

Plaidy, Jean. *St. Thomas's Eve.* **Putnam, 1970.**
About Sir Thomas More, English Chancellor in the time of Henry VIII, and the moral and political conflict between them.

Plaidy, Jean. *Spanish bridegroom.* **Putnam, 1971.**
By one of England's leading writers of historical fiction, this novel deals with the marriage of Mary I of England and Philip II of Spain. Both the characters and their times are the essence of drama.

Ponsonby, Doris. *If my arms could hold.* **Liveright, 1947.**
A romantic story of three sisters with an ambitious mother in 18th century Bath during the era of Beau Nash.

Prescott, Hilda. *Man on a donkey.* **Macmillan, 1952.**
Exceptionally fine novel of life in the England of Henry VIII. Although long, it is filled with fascinating scenes and characters.

Price, Jeramie. *Katrina.* **Farrar, 1955.**
Novel about Peter the Great and Catherine of Russia, realistic and interesting.

Pugh, John. *Captain of the Medici.* **Little, 1953.**
Light melodrama about a blacksmith's son who became a military commander in 16th century Florence.

Pugh, John. *High carnival.* **Little, 1959.**
Long novel of suspense, intrigue and sinister plots set in 16th century Venice.

Rogers, Garet. *Lancet.* **Putnam, 1956.**
Novel of 18th century London, centering around the Hunter brothers, important medical discoverers of the period. Realistic, rather gruesome, but very interesting.

Sabatini, Rafael. *The gamester.* **Houghton, 1949.**
Not so melodramatic as his earlier novels, this tells about John Law, the Scotch financial genius who turned the French economy upside down about 1720.

Sabatini, Rafael. *Sword of Islam.* **Houghton, 1939.**
Cloak-and-dagger tale of 16th century Italy.

Sanders, Joan. *Baneful sorceries.* **Houghton, 1969.**
Gripping story of 17th century France, in which diabolism and witchcraft are important parts.

Sanders, John. *A firework for Oliver.* **Walker, 1965.**
Spy-thriller set in the period of Cromwell. Swashbuckling and racy action.

Schmitt, Gladys. *Rembrandt.* **Random, 1961.**
Long, thorough and engrossing biographical novel.

Schoonover, Lawrence. *The chancellor.* **Little, 1960.**
A romance set in Renaissance France at the beginning of the 16th century. Vivid historical background.

Schoonover, Lawrence. *Key of gold.* **Little, 1968.**
Story of a family of physicians over several generations in the 16th and 17th centuries in Europe and America.

Schoonover, Lawrence. *Prisoner of Tordesillas.* **Little, 1959.**
Picture of European court intrigue centering around mad Queen Juana of Spain, daughter of Ferdinand and Isabella.

Scott, Virgil. *I, John Mordaunt.* **Harcourt, 1964.**
Viscount Mordaunt was an active Royalist during the English Civil War. This novel is a fine one based on his adventures conspiring against the Cromwellians.

Seton, Anya. *Devil water.* **Houghton, 1962.**
Set partly in England and partly in frontier Virginia, the story deals chiefly with the Jacobite rebellions of 1715 and 1745.

Sheean, Vincent. *Day of battle.* **Doubleday, 1938.**
The battle is that at Fontenoy in 1745; the novel encompasses not only that but scenes of the court of Louis XV and Pompadour.

Shellabarger, Samuel. *King's cavalier.* **Little, 1949.**
Good historical romance about a young man who serves his king, Francis I of France, during the Bourbon conspiracy in 1523.

Shellabarger, Samuel. *Lord Vanity.* **Little, 1953.**
Picaresque novel of an 18th century adventurer whose escapades range from Venice to Paris, London, Bath and America. Good historical settings.

Shepard, Odell and Willard. *Jenkin's ear.* **Macmillan, 1951.**
An unusual novel, purportedly written by Horace Walpole and recounting the stories told at his home by several friends regarding how the war of the title had affected them.

Siegel, Benjamin. *A kind of justice.* **Harcourt, 1960.**
A Spanish Jew comes to London just before the Spanish threat of 1588. He is in trouble both as a Spaniard and a Jew. Adventure, vivid picture of the times.

Singer, Isaac. *The slave.* **Farrar, 1962.**
A young 17th century Polish Jew is slave to a Polish peasant and runs away with his daughter. Their efforts to avoid punishment and to find peace and happiness comprise the plot.

Spinatelli, Carl. *Baton sinister.* **Little, 1959.**
Cloak-and-dagger novel of intrigue in 16th century Italy.

Stacton, David. *Dancer in darkness.* **Pantheon, 1962.**
A modern rendering of the Elizabethan tragedy by Webster about the Duchess of Amalfi and her scheming brothers who sought to thwart her love affair.

Stacton, David. *People of the book.* **Putnam, 1965.**
The Thirty Years War is the setting, and there is much action, horror and blood-curdling description. The Swedish chancellor, Oxenstierna, is a principal character.

Stephan, Ruth. *The flight.* **Knopf, 1956.**
An imagined autobiography of Christina, Queen of Sweden in the 17th century, who abdicated to take up a religious life.

Stephan, Ruth. *My crown, my love.* **Knopf, 1960.**
A powerful and absorbing novel about the later years of Queen Christina of Sweden; an excellent picture of 17th century Europe.

Stephens, Eve. *All the Queen's men.* **Crowell, 1960.**
Novel about Elizabeth I and her relationships with the Earl of Leicester, the war with Spain, and the problem of Mary of Scotland.

Stevenson, John P. *Captain general.* **Doubleday, 1956.**
Cloak-and-dagger action in this tale dealing with the Duke of Alba's efforts to stamp out rebellion in the Spanish Netherlands in the 16th century.

Stone, Irving. *The agony and the ecstasy.* **Doubleday, 1961.**
Very long novel depicting in massive detail the fabulous career of Michelangelo.

Stubbs, Jean. *My grand enemy*. Stein & Day, 1967.
Vivid account of a true murder case in England in 1752.

Sutcliff, Rosemary. *Lady in waiting*. Coward, 1957.
Romantic novel about Raleigh and especially his patient wife in a colorful era.

Sutcliff, Rosemary. *Rider on a white horse*. Coward, 1959.
Story about Lady Anne Fairfax, who accompanied her husband's campaigns with Cromwell in the English Civil War.

Taylor, Winchcombe. *Ram*. St. Martins, 1960.
Set in the early 18th century in England, then India and America, this is a long exciting story of a young man's many adventures.

Tessin, Brigitte von. *The bastard*. McKay, 1958.
Very long novel of a French nobleman and his three sons in 16th century France. The religious wars provide a colorful setting.

Thompson, Morton. *The cry and the covenant*. Doubleday, 1949.
Excellent serious novel about a Viennese physician who devoted his career to trying to convince others of the need for preventing puerperal fever.

Tolstoi, Aleksei. *Peter the First*. Macmillan, 1959.
A long and rather complicated novel in the Russian manner. Very graphic pictures of Russian life at many levels in Peter's time.

Trease, Geoffrey. *Snared nightingale*. Vanguard, 1958.
Young Englishman, raised in the household of an Italian nobleman, inherits estate in England and contends with jealous relatives.

Turton, Godfrey. *My Lord of Canterbury*. Doubleday, 1967.
Told in the first person, this is a biography of Thomas Cranmer in fictional form.

Van Dorp, Jan. *Sable lion.* **Putnam, 1954.**
17th century Flemish pirates prey on shipping in the English Channel.

Vining, Elizabeth G. *Take heed of loving me.* **Lippincott, 1963.**
This is the story of the poet John Donne and his marriage to Ann More. Although fictionalized, it is good history, and an interesting interpretation of Donne. Period: the early 1600's.

Walpole, Hugh. *Bright pavilions.* **Macmillan, 1940.**
A chronicle of his Herries family, this time set in the period of Elizabeth I, with Mary of Scotland her rival.

Walsh, Maurice. *Dark rose.* **Stokes, 1938.**
Colorful and romantic novel about the Scottish religious fighting in 1644 and 1645.

Waltari, Mika. *The wanderer.* **Putnam, 1951.**
A sequel to *The Adventurer.* The 16th century hero's activities are in North Africa and among the Turks.

Westcott, Jan. *Queen's grace.* **Crown, 1959.**
Story about Catherine Parr, the sixth wife and surviving widow of Henry VIII.

Wheelwright, Jere. *Wolfshead.* **Scribner, 1949.**
John Aumarle becomes an outlaw and pirate during the reign of Mary I.

White, Leslie T. *Highland hawk.* **Crown, 1952.**
Story of Cromwell's attempts to win the Scottish Highlanders over to the Puritan side.

White, Max. *In the blazing light.* **Duell, 1946.**
Colorful picture of 18th century Spain and especially of the famous artist Goya.

Wilkins, William V. *Fanfare for a witch.* **Macmillan, 1954.**
Melodramatic story about George II, his eldest son, Frederick, and
an improbable Moroccan empress.

Williams, Jay. *Rogue from Padua.* **Little, 1952.**
Picaresque tale of a wandering charlatan who becomes involved in
shady affairs in Germany during the Lutheran Reformation and
peasants' wars, but finally achieves respectability.

Williams, Jay. *The witches.* **Random, 1957.**
Fast-paced novel, set in 16th century Scotland, about a plot, sup-
posedly by witches, against the life of King James VI. Based on
fact, it is a good cloak-and-dagger tale.

Zara, Louis. *Against this rock.* **Creative Age, 1943.**
A vivid picture of Charles V, King of Spain, and of the vast realm
he ruled in the 16th century.

Zara, Louis. *In the house of the king.* **Crown, 1952.**
Biographical novel of the life of Philip II of Spain.

JUVENILE

Bailey, Ralph. *Sea hawks of empire.* **Dutton, 1948.**
Story based on adventures in the search for the Northwest passage,
the defeat of the Armada and other events at sea. Historical background is good.

Bartos-Hoppner, B. *The Cossacks.* **Walck, 1963.**
Story of Mitya, a Russian boy who joins the Cossacks in the time
of Ivan the Terrible.

Beatty, John. *Royal dirk.* **Morrow, 1966.**
Good adventure story of a boy who befriends Bonnie Prince Charlie
and his cause.

Beatty, John and Patricia. *At the Seven Stars.* **Macmillan, 1962.**
Exciting adventures of a Pennsylvania boy in London in the 18th century. Samuel Johnson, Hogarth, the Jacobite rebellion and other historical background.

Bentley, Phyllis. *Adventures of Tom Leigh.* **Doubleday, 1966.**
About an 18th century Yorkshire boy and the newly-born cloth-weaving industry.

Bentley, Phyllis. *Forgery!* **Doubleday, 1968.**
Story of two boys in 18th century Yorkshire who have ethical problems to solve because the father of one of them is a forger and coin-clipper.

Bill, Alfred. *Ring of danger.* **Knopf, 1948.**
Intrigue and danger, and a poison ring, make this an exciting story of a young girl's part in Elizabethan plots.

Cawley, Winifred. *Down the long stairs.* **Holt, 1965.**
Good historical background in this story of a boy who joins the Royalist forces in the English Civil War.

Chute, Marchette. *Wonderful winter.* **Dutton, 1954.**
Good story of a young English heir who runs away from home to London and becomes close friends with Shakespeare and his group.

Coblentz, Catherine. *Bells of Leydon sing.* **Longmans, 1944.**
Story about the Pilgrims in Holland up to their voyage to America.

Daringer, Helen. *Debbie of the Green Gate.* **Harcourt, 1950.**
A story for girls about a girl member of the Pilgrim community in Holland shortly before it left for America.

Daringer, Helen. *Pilgrim Kate.* **Harcourt, 1949.**
Story of a girl who was one of the Pilgrim group living in Scrooby, England. Good background.

De La Torre, Lillian. *White rose of Stuart.* **Nelson, 1954.**
A stirring fictionalized biography of Flora MacDonald, the heroine of Prince Charlie's effort to regain the British throne in 1745.

Eyre, Katherine. *Another spring.* **Oxford U. P., 1949.**
Fictionalized biography of Lady Jane Grey, the nine-day queen. Romantic story for girls.

Gladd, Arthur. *Galleys east!* **Dodd, 1961.**
An adventure story for boys about 16th century sponge-diving, galley warfare and the struggle of Europe against Turkey, ending with the Battle of Lepanto.

Gray, Elizabeth. *I will adventure.* **Viking, 1962.**
Story of a boy in late 16th century London who meets Shakespeare and learns about the theatre.

Habeck, Fritz. *Days of danger.* **Harcourt, 1963.**
About a boy who became involved in the defence of Vienna against the Turks in 1683. Much action and adventure.

Harnett, Cynthia. *Stars of fortune.* **Putnam, 1956.**
Novel particularly good for teen-agers, about Queen Elizabeth I who in her young days was supposed to have been hidden from her enemies in Sulgrave Manor, the home of the Washingtons.

Haycraft, Molly C. *Too near the throne.* **Lippincott, 1959.**
Excellent novel about Lady Arbella Stuart and the intrigues of the courts of Elizabeth I and James I.

Hill, Frank E. *King's company.* **Dodd, 1950.**
Good story of an English boy who leaves home to go to London and work with Shakespeare and his theatrical friends. Useful story for high school.

Hoffman, Eleanor. *Lion of Barbary.* **Holiday, 1947.**
Exciting story of 17th century England and of North Africa, as an English boy seeks to rescue a girl captured by Moorish pirates.

Hunter, Mollie. *The Lothian run.* **Funk & Wagnalls, 1970.**
Romance, adventure and mystery in Edinburgh in 1736. Involves smuggling and political plots with much villainy.

Kirtland, G. B. *One day in Elizabethan England.* **Harcourt, 1962.**
Vivid and interestingly detailed picture of a wealthy English family.

Knight, Ruth. *Search for galleon's gold.* **McGraw, 1956.**
Adventure story about the Armada's gold.

Koningsberger, Hans. *Golden keys.* **Rand McNally, 1956.**
Young Dutchman sails on two historic voyages with the explorer Barents. Good presentation of the early problems of navigation and seamanship.

Kyle, Elisabeth. *Portrait of Lisette.* **Nelson, 1963.**
Fictional biography of a young woman artist in the court of Marie Antoinette.

Kyle, Elisabeth. *Story of Grizel.* **Nelson, 1961.**
Good story of a 17th century Scottish girl whose adventures in the cause of freedom of worship bring excitement and romance.

Meyer, Edith. *Pirate queen.* **Little, 1961.**
Story, based on fact, of a young Irish woman in the Elizabethan period who became head of her clan and led raids on British ships.

Oliver, Jane. *Queen most fair.* **St. Martins, 1960.**
Mary, Queen of Scots, imprisoned in an island castle of the Earl of Douglas, is aided by two children.

Oliver, Jane. *Watch for the morning.* **St. Martins, 1964.**
Novel centering around the controversy over Tyndale's translation of the Bible in the reign of Henry VIII. Adventures of two boys who befriend Tyndale.

Peart, Hendry. *Loyal Grenvilles.* **Knopf, 1958.**
Intrigue and adventure during the struggle between Cromwell and the Royalists.

Picard, Barbara. *Young pretenders.* **Criterion, 1966.**
Story of two English children who become involved in the Rebellion of 1745 and with Prince Charlie.

Polland, Madeleine. *Queen without crown.* **Holt, 1966.**
Powerful and gripping story of Irish versus English in the days of Elizabeth I.

Polland, Madeleine. *White twilight.* **Holt, 1965.**
Story of two young people in 16th century Denmark.

Ritchie, Rita. *Enemy at the gate.* **Dutton, 1959.**
The Turkish siege of Vienna in the 16th century provides the plot and action for this story. Interesting information on early guns.

Softly, Barbara. *Place mill.* **St. Martins, 1963.**
About a boy and his sister caught up in the English Civil war.

Softly, Barbara. *A stone in a pool.* **St. Martins, 1964.**
Story of a boy and girl involved in spying and witchcraft on the Isle of Wight during the 17th century conflict between Puritans and Royalists.

Sprague, Rosemary. *Dance for a diamond star.* **Walck, 1959.**
Story of a young ballerina at the court of Louis XV who must choose between her career and romance. Good background.

Trease, Geoffrey. *Silken secret.* **Vanguard, 1954.**
Story of adventures of a boy in 18th century England.

Trease, Geoffrey. *Trumpets in the west.* **Harcourt, 1947.**
England in the late 17th century, and three youngsters who go to London to seek their fortunes.

Treece, Henry. *Further adventures of Robinson Crusoe.* **Criterion, 1958.**
The author invents a new and interesting sequel to Defoe's tale, in which Crusoe and Friday search for pirate treasure.

Watson, Sally. *Witch of the glens.* **Viking, 1962.**
Story of a 17th century gypsy girl involved in the religious wars in Scotland.

Weir, Rosemary. *Star and the flame.* **Farrar, 1964.**
England at the time of the Great Plague and the Great Fire.

Welch, Ronald. *Captain of dragoons.* **Oxford U. P., 1957.**
Espionage and military adventures of a British officer serving Marlborough at the beginning of the 18th century.

Welch, Ronald. *For the king.* **Criterion, 1962.**
Exciting adventures of a youth fighting in the English Civil War.

Wibberley, Leonard. *Secret of the Hawk.* **Pellegrini & Cudahy, 1952.**
An exciting story written around the slave trade between England and Africa in the 18th century.

Williams, Jay. *Sword and the scythe.* **Oxford U. P., 1946.**
Peasant revolt in Germany in the 16th century.

Wood, James P. *The queen's most honorable pirate.* **Harper, 1961.**
Adventure and action in the company of Sir Francis Drake.

EUROPE, 1789-1914

Abrahams, William. *Imperial waltz.* **Dial, 1954.**
Romantic novel about the Empress Elizabeth of Austria, wife of Franz Joseph.

Aerde, Rogier van. *The tormented.* **Doubleday, 1960.**
A biographical novel about the life of the 19th century French poet, Paul Verlaine. Excellent background.

Almedingen, E. M. *The ladies of St. Hedwig's.* **Vanguard, 1967.**
Conflict between the Polish nuns of a St. Petersburg nunnery and the Russian authorities in the 1860's.

Andric, Ivo. *Bosnian chronicle.* **Knopf, 1963.**
Excellent novel by a Nobel Prize winner. The setting is Bosnia about 1807; two consuls, one French and one Austrian, confront each other in a wild and hostile environment.

Andric, Ivo. *Bridge on the Drina.* **Macmillan, 1959.**
Written by a distinguished Bosnian author, this sweeping novel depicts a Bosnian town and its 300-year old bridge over a period of many years up to World War I, when the bridge was destroyed.

Anthony, Evelyn. *Far flies the eagle.* **Crowell, 1955.**
Graphic novel about Czar Alexander I of Russia and the events of his time.

Anthony, Evelyn. *Victoria and Albert.* **Crowell, 1958.**
Well-done fictional account of the love affair that ended tragically, and of England in mid-century.

Aragon, Louis. *Holy week.* **Putnam, 1961.**
A panorama and thorough picture of events in France just before Easter in 1815, as Napoleon returned from Elba to Paris and Louis XVIII fled toward Belgium.

Ashton, Helen. *Footman in powder.* **Dodd, 1954.**
Story about a royal servant in Brighton in the late 1700's and early 1800's. The picture of Brighton and its colorful activities is vivid and authentic.

Biely, Andrey. *St. Petersburg.* **Grove, 1959.**
Excellent novel of the revolutionary year of 1905. Drama, suspense, and wit all play a part.

Bolton, Guy. *The Olympians.* **World, 1961.**
Novel based on the romance of Shelley and Mary Godwin.

Bonnet, Theodore. *The mudlark.* **Doubleday, 1949.**
A delightful story of a London waif who managed to get into Windsor Castle in Victoria's time, and thereby started a chain of important events.

Born, Edith de. *Felding castle.* **Knopf, 1959.**
Recollections of her girlhood told by an artistic woman in pre-World War I Austria.

Brenner, Jacques. *Nephew to the emperor.* **World, 1959.**
Beethoven is the "emperor" of the title, and his career is the main theme of this novel.

Buckmaster, Henrietta. *Fire in the heart.* **Harcourt, 1948.**
A biographical novel about the career of the noted actress, Fanny Kemble.

Carr, John Dickson. *Captain Cut-throat.* **Harper, 1955.**
One of this author's exciting historical-mystery novels. The setting is in 1805, when Napoleon's army was preparing to invade England. The mysterious murders of French sentries provide the plot.

Chapman, Hester. *Eugénie.* **Little, 1961.**
Good biographical novel set around the life of Napoleon III's Empress, and her influence on the fashions and society of the time.

Chapman, Hester. *Fear no more.* **Reynal, 1968.**
Novel written around the tragic and mysterious life of the young son of Louis XVI, who became the lost Dauphin.

Clevely, Hugh. *Stranger in two worlds.* **Appleton, 1959.**
Adventure and romance in 19th century Ireland, London, and Chicago at the time of the great fire.

Coker, Elizabeth. *La Belle.* **Dutton, 1959.**
Glamor and greed mark this story of the career of Marie Boozer, who started as a camp-follower for Sherman's army and eventually became the toast of world capitals.

Cordell, Alexander. *Rape of the fair country.* **Doubleday, 1959.**
Powerful story of the struggle of Welsh workers in the 1830's against the brutality of the iron masters and near-slave labor system.

Cordell, Alexander. *Song of the earth.* **Simon & Schuster, 1969.**
A novel of 19th century Wales and the lives and problems of the workers in the coal mining industry.

Coryn, Marjorie. *Good-bye, my son.* **Appleton, 1943.**
A novel of interest, dealing with the Bonaparte family and particularly with the mother of that remarkable group.

Costain, Thomas B. *The last love.* **Doubleday, 1963.**
Romantic, semi-factual novel about Napoleon's close friendship with an English girl living on St. Helena.

Costain, Thomas B. *The Tontine.* **Doubleday, 1955.**
A very long two-volume novel about several generations of two English Victorian families. Many characters and a plot building well to a climax.

Dane, Clemence. *He brings great news.* **Random, 1945.**
A novel of how a British naval officer brought the news of the victory at Trafalgar back to England.

Davis, Harold. *Harp of a thousand strings.* **Morrow, 1947.**
A novel of the French Revolution and the Barbary War, set mostly in Tripoli. Very well-written.

Delderfield, R. F. *God is an Englishman.* **Simon & Schuster, 1970.**
Enjoyable novel of English family life in the 19th century.

Delderfield, R. F. *A horseman riding by.* **Simon & Schuster, 1967.**
A very long but interesting novel about the lives of people in rural Devonshire in the time of Edward VII.

Delderfield, R. F. *Seven men of Gascony.* **Bobbs, 1949.**
A novel of the Napoleonic Wars and of how they affected a group of ordinary men.

Delves-Broughton, Josephine. *Officer and gentleman.* **McGraw, 1951.**
A colorful picture of military pageantry in England and Russia at the time of the Crimean War.

Denti di Pirajno, Alberto. *Ippolita.* **Doubleday, 1961.**
Story of the life of an aristocratic Italian woman of the early 19th century, who in her later years becomes almost insanely avaricious. Well-written.

Du Maurier, Daphne. *The glass-blowers.* **Doubleday, 1963.**
Story of a French family in the glass industry who migrate to London during the French Revolution. Based on actual letters, it gives a realistic picture of the period.

Du Maurier, Daphne. *Jamaica Inn.* **Doubleday, 1936.**
A story of sinister doings in Cornwall in the early 1800's, with wreckers, smugglers and eventually romance.

Eaton, Evelyn. *Give me your golden hand.* **Farrar, 1951.**
A novel of adventure and intrigue about an illegitimate son of George III.

Eden, Dorothy. *Lady of Mallow.* **Coward, 1962.**
Romantic melodrama of the 1800's dealing with the ownership of a large English estate. Action and mystery.

Endore, Guy. *King of Paris.* **Simon & Schuster, 1956.**
Highly fictionalized life of Alexander Dumas. As history it is unreliable, but it makes a flamboyant story.

Forester, C. S. *Beat to quarters.* **Little, 1937.**
First of the notable series of sea stories featuring Horatio Hornblower.

Forester, C. S. *Commodore Hornblower*. Little, 1945.
Fascinating volume in the saga of Hornblower, who here works successfully to keep Sweden and Russia on Britain's side against Napoleon.

Forester, C. S. *Flying colours*. Little, 1938.
One of the inimitable Hornblower stories of the Napoleonic Wars.

Forester, C. S. *Hornblower and the Atropos*. Little, 1952.
This volume in the Hornblower saga deals with an early part of his career, and includes the usual quota of excitement and realistic adventure.

Forester, C. S. *Hornblower and the Hotspur*. Little, 1962.
One part of the famous series of sea stories, this describes the hero's adventures that led to his promotion as capatin.

Forester, C. S. *Lord Hornblower*. Little, 1946.
This popular figure here reaches the apogee of his success in the Napoleonic Wars.

Forester, C. S. *Ship of the line*. Little, 1938.
Captain Hornblower commands a ship on blockade off Spain during the Napoleonic Wars.

Fraser, George M. *Flashman*. World, 1969.
An amusing and very readable tour-de-force, this purports to be the autobiography of Flashman, the noted bully in *Tom Brown's School-days*. He describes his later adventures in the army during the Crimean War and in Afghanistan; always he takes pride in the most caddish conduct.

Frye, Pearl. *Game for empires*. Little, 1950.
A novel about the career of Admiral Nelson during the war with France, well-told.

Frye, Pearl. *Sleeping sword.* **Little, 1952.**
Novel about Lord Nelson and Emma Hamilton, although naval action is more important than romance.

Gavin, Catherine. *Madeleine.* **St. Martins, 1957.**
Romantic novel of the period of Napoleon III and the Suez crisis.

Gennari, Genevieve. *Riven heart.* **McKay, 1956.**
Romance of the Napoleonic and Bourbon restoration periods.

Gerson, Noel. *Emperor's ladies.* **Doubleday, 1959.**
Court romance about Napoleon's empress Marie Louise and this exciting period of French history.

Gibbs, Willa. *The dedicated.* **Morrow, 1960.**
The career of Edward Jenner and the bitter controversies about how to prevent smallpox. Early 19th century England.

Gibbs, Willa. *Seed of mischief.* **Farrar, 1953.**
A story of the French Revolution and particularly of Louis XVII, the lost Dauphin.

Gibbs, Willa. *Tell your sons.* **Farrar, 1946.**
A long novel about Napoleon and of the almost hypnotic loyalty he created in many people.

Gibbs, Willa. *The twelfth physician.* **Farrar, 1954.**
Set in the period of the Revolution in France, this portrays the problems of a young doctor trying to determine where his duties lie.

Giono, Jean. *Horseman on the roof.* **Knopf, 1952.**
The adventures of an ex-hussar and a lady making their way through Provence in 1838 amid a plague-ridden countryside.

Gorman, Herbert. *Brave general.* **Farrar, 1942.**
A story about General Boulanger, the political opportunist and popular hero of Paris in the 1880's.

Gorman, Herbert. *Mountain and the plain.* **Farrar, 1936.**
Full and dramatic novel about the earlier years of the French Revolution, and the great figures of the Jacobin leaders.

Graham, Winston. *Demelza.* **Doubleday, 1953.**
A sequel to an earlier novel, *The Renegade.* It tells of the people of the Cornish coasts in 1788-1790, when life there was harsh and brutal.

Grun, Bernard. *Golden quill.* **Putnam, 1956.**
The life of Mozart purportedly told in the diary of his sister.

Hauser, Marianne. *Prince Ishmael.* **Stein & Day, 1963.**
A re-creation of the story of Caspar Hauser, the mystery boy of Nuremberg in 1828; attempts to describe how the world appeared to someone whose whole previous life had been spent in solitary confinement.

Herbert, Alan. *Why Waterloo?* **Doubleday, 1952.**
Highly interesting and well-written novel about Napoleon from Elba to Waterloo.

Heyer, Georgette. *A civil contract.* **Putnam, 1961.**
About a marriage of convenience set against the background of Regency England.

Heyer, Georgette. *False colours.* **Dutton, 1964.**
Comedy of manners and society in Regency England.

Heyer, Georgette. *Grand Sophy.* **Putnam, 1950.**
One of this author's entertaining and highly authentic stories of Regency London.

Heyer, Georgette. *An infamous army.* **Doubleday, 1938.**
Well-written novel of Napoleon's hundred days and its climax at Waterloo, as seen by a group of British aristocrats in Brussels.

Heyer, Georgette. *Pistols for two.* **Dutton, 1964.**
Collection of eleven short stories, all set in the period of the Regency
in England. Light but enjoyable tales.

Heyer, Georgette. *Spanish bride.* **Doubleday, 1940.**
Romance and vivid military action in the Peninsular campaigns of
the Napoleonic Wars.

Heyer, Georgette. *Sylvester.* **Putnam, 1958.**
Romantic complications in the setting of Regency England.

Heyer, Georgette. *Toll-gate.* **Putnam, 1954.**
Romance and adventure in this Regency England tale about a young
aristocrat who, lost on the moors, comes to a toll-gate and helps its
young keeper.

Heyer, Georgette. *Unknown Ajax.* **Putnam, 1960.**
Another of this author's entertaining romances about the Darracott
family in Regency England.

Heyer, Georgette. *Venetia.* **Putnam, 1959.**
Light romantic plotting in England of the early 1800's.

Hodge, Jane. *Maulever Hall.* **Doubleday, 1964.**
Mystery, a case of amnesia, and romance in the aristocratic circles
of England around 1830. Good Gothic-type tale.

Howells, J. Harvey. *Bide me fair.* **Simon & Schuster, 1968.**
A warm and well-written story of a Scottish family at the turn of
the century.

Jennings, John. *Banners against the wind.* **Little, 1954.**
Story based on the career of Dr. Samuel Gridley Howe, especially
in his participation in the Greek war of independence in 1824.

Johnson, David. *Proud canaries.* **Sloane, 1959.**
Vigorous story of a cavalryman in Napoleon's armies, and his many adventures.

Johnston, Myrtle. *The rising.* **Appleton, 1939.**
Vivid novel about the Irish Fenian rebellion against the British in 1867.

Jordan, Mildred. *Asylum for the queen.* **Knopf, 1948.**
Story of the French Revolution. Young artistocrat, hoping to save Marie Antoinette, comes to America to prepare a refuge for her. When the queen dies, he returns to France.

Kazantzakes, Nikos. *Freedom or death.* **Simon & Schuster, 1955.**
Long and violent book about the struggle of the people of Crete against Turkish rule in 1889.

Kennedy, Margaret. *A night in Cold Harbor.* **Macmillan, 1960.**
A picture of an English village and gentle society in the early 19th century.

Kent, Alexander. *Form line of battle.* **Putnam, 1969.**
Thrilling naval adventure in the British attempt to capture Toulon in 1793.

Kenyon, Frank. *Emma.* **Crowell, 1955.**
Romantic novel about Lady Hamilton, the mistress of Admiral Nelson.

Lampedusa, Giuseppe di. *The leopard.* **Pantheon, 1960.**
A highly-praised novel of a noble Sicilian family during the period from 1860 to 1910.

Leslie, Doris. *The Prime Minister's wife.* **Doubleday, 1961.**
Biographical novel of Mary Anne Disraeli.

Lewis, Paul. *The Nelson touch.* **Holt, 1960.**
Interesting portrait of Lord Nelson, with the emphasis more on his
romantic problems than his naval exploits.

Lincoln, Victoria. *Charles.* **Little, 1961.**
A biographical novel of Dickens, his times and his personal problems.
A good revelation of the novelist as a person.

Lindop, Audrey. *Way to the lantern.* **Doubleday, 1961.**
Adventure story about an English actor who is forced, for romantic
reasons, to go to Paris during the Terror.

Lodi, Maria. *Charlotte Morel — the dream.* **Putnam, 1970.**
A novel of romance and political activity in the last days of Napoleon
III's empire, when revolution was close at hand.

Lofts, Norah. *Afternoon of an autocrat.* **Doubleday, 1956.**
Period piece set in an English manor at the end of the 18th century.

Lofts, Norah. *Bless this house.* **Doubleday, 1954.**
An unusual and fascinating book, recounting eight episodes in as
many generations of the existence of a single English countryhouse
over four centuries.

Macken, Walter. *The silent people.* **Macmillan, 1962.**
The struggle of the Irish to survive the potato famine and political
oppression in the early 19th century.

Malamud, Bernard. *The fixer.* **Farrar, 1966.**
Excellent novel, set in Kiev in 1913, of a Russian Jew accused of
murder and tortured for a confession. His refusal to be conquered
symbolizes the struggle between character and power.

Manceron, Claude. *So brief a spring.* **Putnam, 1957.**
Well-written and vivid story of Paris in the period between
Napoleon's return from Elba and the Battle of Waterloo.

Martin, Sylvia. *I, Madame Tussaud.* **Harper, 1956.**
The colorful story of Ann Marie Gresholtz who as Madame Tussaud became a famous figure in France and England in the Napoleonic era.

McKenney, Ruth. *Mirage.* **Farrar, 1956.**
Colorful and action-packed novel about Napoleon's campaign in Egypt. To be read more for entertainment than serious history.

Morris, Ira Jefferies. *The rake and the rebel.* **Morrow, 1967.**
Romance and adventure during the Napoleonic Wars, especially in Russia.

Neill, Robert. *Mills of Colne.* **Doubleday, 1959.**
Romance set in 19th century England, descriptive of the early effects of the Industrial Revolution.

Neumann, Alfred. *Another Caesar.* **Knopf, 1935.**
Powerful novel of Napoleon III and the Second Empire.

O'Brian, Patrick. *Master and commander.* **Lippincott, 1969.**
The ambitious captain of a British brig during the Napoleonic wars, his first mate and his ship's doctor are the protagonists of this lively novel of naval warfare.

O'Flaherty, Liam. *Famine.* **Random, 1937.**
Powerful and dramatic picture of Ireland in the 1840's.

Pidoll, Carl von. *Eroica.* **Vanguard, 1957.**
Good fictionalized account of Beethoven's career.

Plunkett, James. *Strumpet city.* **Delacorte, 1969.**
Novel of people of the Dublin slums about 1907. Realistic and engrossing.

Pope, Dudley. *Drumbeat.* **Doubleday, 1967.**
Rousing tale of naval warfare during the Napoleonic Wars — a sequel to *Ramage* (q.v.).

Pope, Dudley. *Ramage.* **Lippincott, 1965.**
Exciting story of a British naval officer's adventures in the Napoleonic wars, *a la* C. S. Forester.

Postgate, Raymond. *Every man is God.* **Simon & Schuster, 1960.**
A Victorian period piece about a family playing out a Greek-type tragedy.

Powers, Anne. *The thousand fires.* **Bobbs, 1957.**
Romance and battle action during the last five years of the Napoleonic wars.

Pratolini, Vasco. *Metello.* **Little, 1967.**
Portrays the Italian working class labor movement in Florence about 1902.

Rayner, Denys. *The long fight.* **Holt, 1958.**
Exciting account, based on fact, of a three-day battle between a French and a British ship in the Indian Ocean in 1808.

Read, Miss. *The market square.* **Houghton, 1967.**
Charming tale of small English village life in the early 20th century.

Rhys, Jean. *Wide Sargasso Sea.* **Norton, 1967.**
Set in Jamaica and England in the 1830's, this novel deals with the early life of a Charlotte Bronte character from *Jane Eyre*.

Roberto, Federico de. *The viceroys.* **Harcourt, 1962.**
A long novel originally published in Italian in 1894, this is a story of a powerful Sicilian family in the mid-19th century who hold their arrogance and influence through every political and social change.

Rudigoz, Roger. *French dragoon.* **Coward, 1959.**
After Napoleon's abdication one of his cavalry officers tries to return to civilian life only to run afoul of the police of the new regime.

Schwarz-Bart, Andre. *Last of the just.* **Atheneum, 1960.**
A powerful and artistic novel encompassing the tragedy of European Jewry over eight centuries, depicted in successive members of one family.

Sciascia, Leonardo. *The council of Egypt.* **Knopf, 1966.**
The setting is Sicily in the late 18th century; efforts to overthrow the Bourbon monarchy there.

Selinko, Annemarie. *Désirée.* **Morrow, 1952.**
A Napoleonic novel, dealing chiefly with Bernadotte, who became king of Sweden.

Shay, Edith and Smith, Katherine. *Private adventure of Captain Shaw.* **Houghton, 1945.**
A witty and entertaining story of a young Cape Cod sea captain who finds himself in Paris during the Reign of Terror.

Singer, Isaac B. *The manor.* **Farrar, 1967.**
Describes the life of an "emancipated" Jewish family in Poland in the late 19th century.

Smith, Vian. *The wind blows free.* **Doubleday, 1968.**
Shows the effects of the enclosure process in early 19th century England on various classes of people from great land-owners to tenants.

Solomon, Ruth F. *Candlesticks and the Cross.* **Putnam, 1967.**
Good novel of wealthy Russian Jewess who gives up her non-Jewish husband to save her children from religious persecution. Period just prior to World War I.

Sorenson, Virginia. *Kingdom come.* **Harcourt, 1960.**
Good picture of rural Danish folk in the 1850's, and of their conversion to Mormonism.

Stacton, David. *Sir William.* **Putnam, 1963.**
Set in Naples in the 1790's, this is the story of the triangle of Lord
Nelson, Emma Hamilton and her husband, Sir William.

Steelman, Robert. *Call of the Arctic.* **Coward, 1960.**
Biographical novel on the career of Charles Hall who made three
voyages to the Far North in the 19th century.

Stephens, Eve. *Far flies the eagle.* **Crowell, 1955.**
Fictionalized biography of the Russian Emperor, Alexander I.

Styles, Showell. *His was the fire.* **Vanguard, 1957.**
Good fictionalized biography of Sir John Moore, the fine British
general in the Napoleonic Wars.

Styles, Showell. *The sea officer.* **Macmillan, 1962.**
Describes, with a good deal of fine sea action, the career of Admiral
Edward Pellew, a contemporary of Nelson.

Sundman, Per. *Flight of the Eagle.* **Pantheon, 1970.**
An adventure story which re-creates the 1897 attempt by a Swedish
scientist to reach the North Pole by balloon.

Thirkell, Angela. *Coronation summer.* **Oxford U. P., 1937.**
Clever and fascinating picture of England in 1837, when Victoria
became Queen. The plot is merely the excuse for a wide variety of
graphic details of the period.

Thorndike, Russell and Buchanan, William. *Christopher Syn.* **Abelard,
1960.**
Exciting story about a saintly vicar who is a smuggler by night. The
setting is the marshes of southern England in the late 18th century.

Tickell, Jerrard. *Hussar honeyman.* **Doubleday, 1963.**
Amusing and light romance of two Hungarian officers after the same
girl and the same promotion. Time: 1900. Place: Budapest.

Tilsley, Frank. *Mutiny.* **Reynal, 1959.**
Vivid picture of the harshness of British naval life in the early 1800's.

Tomlinson, H. M. *Morning light.* **Macmillan, 1947.**
Tells of a sea voyage from England to California about 1850, and of social conditions in England at that time.

Troyat, Henri. *Brotherhood of the red poppy.* **Simon & Schuster, 1961.**
Panoramic novel with colorful background of the allied occupation of Paris in 1814.

Waldeck, R. G. *Lustre in the sky.* **Doubleday, 1946.**
About the Congress of Vienna, which followed Napoleon's downfall. Full of pageantry and famous people.

Waring, M. W. *The witnesses.* **Houghton, 1967.**
Set in Russia in the early 20th century, this story provides a picture of the rising discontent, the unheeding aristocracy and the downfall of the old regime.

Werfel, Franz. *Song of Bernadette.* **Viking, 1942.**
The very popular and moving novel which tells the story of Bernadette Soubirous, who in 1858 claimed to have seen a vision of the Virgin.

Wilkins, W. V. *Being met together.* **Macmillan, 1944.**
A long and vigorous melodrama of a young American who, goaded by an English-hating grandmother, goes to France and becomes a Bonapartist agent. Lots of action.

Wilkins, William. *Consort for Victoria.* **Doubleday, 1959.**
Melodramatic novel about a plot to throw doubt on Prince Albert's legitimacy and so blackmail the Queen into renouncing the throne.

Winwar, Frances. *The eagle and the rock.* **Harper, 1952.**
Unusually good and authentic fictional life of Napoleon.

Wright, Constance. *Chance for glory.* **Holt, 1957.**
While this is not really a novel, it is exciting enough for good fiction. It is the story of the attempts to rescue Lafayette from imprisonment in Austria during the French Revolution.

Zilahy, Lajos. *Century in scarlet.* **McGraw, 1964.**
Chronicle of a noble Hungarian family through the period from the Congress of Vienna to the First World War. Pictures all the glitter, pageantry and excitement of the age.

JUVENILE

Benary-Isbert, Margot. *Under a changing moon.* **Harcourt, 1964.**
Enjoyable story of a girl and her family in a southern German town in 1866.

Beyer, Audrey. *Sapphire pendant.* **Knopf, 1961.**
Romance and intrigue in England and France in 1803 during the Napoleonic Wars.

Burton, Hester. *Castors away!* **World, 1963.**
Action-filled story centering around Admiral Nelson's victory over the French at Trafalgar, and the successful efforts of an English family to save the life of a seaman washed ashore from a troopship.

Burton, Hester. *Time of trial.* **World, 1964.**
Story of a girl and her father in England in the early 19th century who became deeply involved in trying to bring about improvement of the slums, and so aroused official anger.

Crisp, Frank. *Treasure of Barbry Swin.* **Coward, 1955.**
Seafaring adventure and villainy involve an English lad on a ship seeking a mysterious treasure in 1804.

Eaton, Jeanette. *Betsy's Napoleon.* **Morrow, 1952.**
The story of the friendship between Napoleon, during his last exile, and a young girl living on St. Helena.

Hunter, Mollie. *The Lothian run.* **Funk, 1970.**
An exciting story about smugglers, gun-battles and riots in early 18th century Edinburgh.

Llewellyn, Richard. *Witch of Merthyn.* **Doubleday, 1954.**
A story about the Welsh in the Napoleonic period, with much local color and romantic appeal.

Malvern, Gladys. *Curtain's at eight.* **Macrae Smith, 1957.**
Story for girls about theatrical life in London in the late 19th century.

Malvern. Gladys. *Stephanie.* **Macrae Smith, 1956.**
Fictional biography of the Empress Josephine's niece, Stephanie de Beauharnais.

McLean, Allan. *Ribbon of fire.* **Harcourt, 1962.**
The scene is the Island of Skye in the 1800's, and the story tells of the crofters' fight against a harsh landlord.

O'Connor, Patrick. *Society of foxes.* **Washburn, 1954.**
Exciting story for boys about the things that happened to a young guard on the Dover mail coach in 1801, when England was fighting Napoleon.

Spencer, Cornelia. *More hands for man.* **Day, 1960.**
About an English family in the late 18th century and how it was affected by the Industrial Revolution. Good historical background.

Stevenson, Anne. *Ralph Dacre.* **Walker, 1967.**
Young romance and adventure in London and northern England in the early 19th century. Good background. For teen-agers especially.

Styles, Showell. *Midshipman Quinn.* **Vanguard, 1958.**
Enjoyable story of a young British midshipman's adventures in the Mediterranean during the Napoleonic wars.

Trease, Geoffrey. *Follow my black plume.* **Vanguard, 1963.**
Good story of an English boy who, while visiting Rome, gets caught up in the revolutionary activities of Garibaldi and joins his forces.

Trease, Geoffrey. *Victory at Valmy.* **Vanguard, 1960.**
Adventure against the background of the French Revolution.

Vance, Marguerite. *The wildling.* **Dutton, 1957.**
The story of Empress Elizabeth of Austria, wife of Francis Joseph.

Welch, Ronald. *Escape from France.* **Criterion, 1961.**
Young Englishman goes to France to try to rescue relatives caught up in the Revolution there. Swashbuckling adventure.

Wibberley, Leonard. *Kevin O'Connor of the Light Brigade.* **Farrar, 1957.**
Rousing story of a young Irishman who joins the British army during the Crimean War.

Williamson, Joanne. *Jacobin's daughter.* **Knopf, 1956.**
Good story of a girl in Revolutionary Paris, with vivid pictures of the Jacobin leaders.

EUROPE, 1914-1939

Amedingen, Martha. *Frossia.* **Harcourt, 1944.**
An unusual novel, full of interesting insights into conditions in Russia before and after the 1917 revolution.

Almedingen, Martha. *Winter in the heart.* **Appleton, 1960.**
A scholarly priest reluctantly goes to a parish in Finland in 1915, where his aloofness and coldness alienate the people. The story describes how they gradually come to understand each other, especially after the Communists take over in 1918.

Angarsky, Andrew. *Eighty-seven days.* **Knopf, 1962.**
A long but well-written and engrossing novel of the unsuccessful anti-Bolshevik movement in Russia in 1918.

Armstrong, Thomas. *A ring has no end.* **Sloane, 1958.**
Vivid picture of Russian society over the period from the Crimean War to the 1917 revolution.

Ballinger, W. A. *Men that God made mad.* **Putman, 1969.**
A violent exciting novel about a group of fighting Irishmen in the Easter Rebellion in Dublin in 1916.

Blankfort, Michael. *Behold the fire.* **New Am. Lib., 1965.**
Novel about a group of Jewish pioneers who, during the First World War, help the British to overthrow Turkish control in Palestine.

Bridge, Ann. *Frontier passage.* **Little, 1942.**
A novel of the Spanish Civil War along the French border. Vivid portrayal.

Buchan, John. *Adventures of Richard Hannay.* **Houghton, 1939.**
Combines in one book three of the best spy and thriller stories of the First World War ever written: *The 39 Steps, Greenmantle,* and *Mr. Standfast.*

Cloete, Stuart. *How young they die.* **Trident, 1969.**
Story of a young British officer in the terrible battles of Ypres and the Somme in the Great War.

Colegate, Isabel. *Statues in a garden.* **Knopf, 1966.**
Portrays an aristocratic British family in early 1914, the unwitting symbol of the end of an era.

Conchon, Georges. *Measure of victory.* **Orion, 1961.**
Two brothers, on opposite sides during the Spanish Civil War, come together after the war and seek to solve the problems of loyalty and kinship.

Condon, Richard. *An infinity of mirrors.* **Random, 1964.**
Exciting novel set in Berlin and Paris from 1932 to 1944, in which the evil of Hitlerism is brought out as the motivating force in the action.

Del Castillo, Michel. *The disinherited.* **Knopf, 1959.**
A novel of the Spanish Civil War, portraying the horrors of useless war.

Djilas, Milovan. *Montenegro.* **Harcourt, 1963.**
Written while the author was in a Yugoslav prison, this is a powerful story centering about the defeat of Montenegro by Austria in 1916 and its eventual absorption by Yugoslavia. The Montenegrin spirit is the real hero.

Dumitriu, Petru. *The prodigals.* **Pantheon, 1963.**
Rumanian aristocratic society during and after the First World War — a picture of decadence and an invitation to Communist overthrow.

Farrell, Michael. *Thy tears might cease.* **Knopf, 1964.**
A very long story of a young Irishman in the early 20th century at the time of the Troubles. Introspective and analytical of character and personality.

Fitzgibbon, Constantine. *High heroic.* **Norton, 1969.**
Novel about the Irish 1916 uprising and particularly about the Irish patriot Michael Collins. Good picture of the period and events.

Foldes, Jolan. *Street of the Fishing Cat.* **Farrar, 1937.**
Story about a group of refugees of several nationalities in Paris just after World War I.

Gann, Ernest K. *In the company of eagles.* **Simon & Schuster, 1966.**
Story of aerial fighting over France in the First World War.

Gironella, Jose Maria. *One million dead.* **Doubleday, 1963.**
Sequel to *The Cypresses Believe in God,* both about the Spanish Civil War. This one deals with the conflict itself, 1936-39, and the various members of a family affected closely by it.

Habe, Hans. *Ilona.* **Harcourt, 1961.**
A woman, her daughter and grandaughter are the chief characters in a panoramic novel of European politics from 1886 to 1956.

Hardman, Ric. *Fifteen flags.* **Little, 1968.**
Long and colorful story written around the allied intervention in Siberia after the First World War.

Harris, John. *Covenant with death.* **Sloane, 1961.**
Describes the organizing of a group of Londoners into a battalion, their training and finally their part in the terrible Battle of the Somme in 1916.

Harris, John. *Light cavalry action.* **Morrow, 1967.**
Tale of action in the Allied Expeditionary Force against the Bolsheviks in 1919. Good realism and excitement.

Hemingway, Ernest. *For whom the bell tolls.* **Scribner, 1940.**
The classic novel of the American Loyalist in the Spanish Civil War, and of the horrors of that tragedy.

Hindus, Maurice. *Sons and fathers.* **Doubleday, 1940.**
Excellent novel of the Russian Revolution, when a father and son represent opposite ideologies. The story is powerful and preaches no sermon ; events speak for themselves.

Hughes, Richard. *Fox in the attic.* **Harper, 1961.**
Excellent study in novel form of the early development of Hitler's influence in Germany.

Hunter, Jack D. *The Blue Max.* **Dutton, 1964.**
Story of an alcoholic German fighter pilot in the First World War.

Johnson, David. *Promenade in Champagne.* **Sloane, 1961.**
Set in World War I, this is a good picture of a group of closely-knit young French officers in the stress of war.

Kessel, Joseph. *The Medici fountain.* **St. Martins, 1963.**
Story about a young student in Paris during World War I.

Koestler, Arthur. *Darkness at noon.* Macmillan, 1941.
Widely-admired novel about the Russian Revolution and the evils of
totalitarianism.

Lofts, Norah. *Calf for Venus.* Doubleday, 1949.
Novel with a smuggling background in early 19th century England.

Lofts, Norah. *Golden fleece.* Knopf, 1944.
Tells of a number of odd things that happened to a group of people
who stayed for a day and night at an English inn in 1817.

Lynam, Shevawn. *Spirit and the clay.* Little, 1954.
Novel about a group of devoutly Catholic Basque peasants who have
their faith severely shaken by the events of the Spanish Civil War.

Macken, Walter. *The scorching wind.* Macmillan, 1964.
Story of two brothers and the divided people of County Galway in
Ireland during the struggle against British rule in the early 1900's.
Fine atmosphere, good action.

Matute, Ana Maria. *School of the sun.* Pantheon, 1962.
About the effects of the divided loyalties of the Spanish Civil War
on the maturing of a young woman.

McCann, Hugh. *"Utmost fish!"* Simon & Schuster, 1965.
Action and adventure in Africa in World War I, as the British move
two large motorboats a thousand miles overland to attack a German
fleet on Lake Tanganyika.

Murciaux, Christian. *The unforsaken.* Pantheon, 1963.
Story of a Spanish peasant youth drawn into the vortex of the
Spanish Civil War. His dilemmas were those of most other
Spaniards.

Murdoch, Iris. *The red and the green.* Viking, 1965.
Story of an Anglo-Irish family in Dublin during the 1916 uprising.
Interesting characters of several types.

Nilin, Pavel. *Comrade Venka.* **Simon & Schuster, 1959.**
Set in a small town in Siberia in the early days of the Communist regime. An interesting story which points up the innate cruelty of party realism in Russia.

O'Flaherty, Liam. *Insurrection.* **Little, 1951.**
Very powerful depiction of the Easter uprising in Dublin in 1916.

Pasternak, Boris. *Doctor Zhivago.* **Pantheon, 1958.**
Widely-acclaimed novel which gives a remarkable picture of Russian life and the problems of humanity.

Peyrefitte, Roger. *Diplomatic diversions.* **Thames, 1953.**
Witty and satirical picture of diplomatic circles in Athens just before the Second World War.

Plowman, Stephanie. *Three lives for the Czar.* **Houghton, 1970.**
Vivid picture of the Imperial Russian Court in the years before the First World War.

Powell, Anthony. *The kindly ones.* **Little, 1962.**
Excellent novel of English people trying to cope with conditions through two World Wars.

Reinhardt, Richard. *Ashes of Smyrna.* **Harper, 1971.**
A very realistic novel of the conflict between Turks and Greeks in Smyrna between 1919 and 1922.

Serge, Victor. *Birth of our power.* **Doubleday, 1966.**
An autobiographical novel, originally published in French in 1931, a powerful portrayal of a revolutionist who moves from Spain to Russia in 1917 to aid the workers' cause.

Shedd, Margaret. *Hosannah tree.* **Doubleday, 1967.**
Story of missionaries in Persia at the time of the First World War. Good action and colorful settings.

Smith, Frederick E. *A killing for the Hawks.* McKay, 1967.
Aerial warfare in World War I, with personal conflict between two
British fighter-pilots.

Zilinsky, Ursula. *Before the glory ended.* Lippincott, 1967.
Novel of aristocracy in Europe as it began its decline between the
two world wars. Romantic novel of manners.

EUROPE, 1939 AND AFTER

Arnold, Elliott. *A night of watching.* Scribner, 1967.
Exciting story of the smuggling of 8000 Danish Jews out of Denmark
by the Resistance forces in 1943.

Bates, H. E. *A moment in time.* Farrar, 1964.
Story about British fighter pilots defending England during the
Battle of Britain.

Beste, R. Vernon. *The moonbeams.* Harper, 1961.
Hard-hitting action among a group of Allied saboteurs in Occupied
France.

Boll, Heinrich. *Adam, where art thou?* Criterion, 1955.
Graphic and realistic novel of the chaotic retreat of a German military unit in the Balkans, and the subsequent fate of some of its
members.

Bridge, Ann. *Place to stand.* Macmillan, 1953.
Romantic adventure novel of a young American socialite who was
living in Budapest when the Nazis came, and who risked her life
helping to protect a stranded Polish family.

Bridge, Ann. *The tightening string.* McGraw, 1961
Problems encountered by members of the British legation in Budapest in the early days of World War II in the face of Nazi conquest.

95

Clavel, Bernard. *Fruits of winter.* **McCann, 1969.**
A French family in occupied France during World War II is divided sharply in its loyalties between collaboration and resistance.

Cochrell, Boyd. *Barren beaches of hell.* **Holt, 1959.**
Experiences of a very young Marine in the South Pacific in World War II.

Crichton, Robert. *The secret of Santa Vittoria.* **Simon & Schuster, 1966.**
Captivating and humorous story of how Italian villagers saved their million bottles of wine from Nazi occupation troops.

Davis, Dorothy and Ross, Jerome. *God speed the night.* **Scribner, 1968.**
Story of a nun who helps a man escape from Nazi-occupied France into Spain during the War.

Davis, Robert. *The Dingle War.* **Prentice, 1968.**
Set in neutral Ireland during World War II, this is a humorous and enjoyable story of interesting people and wartime problems.

Del Castillo, Michel. *Child of our time.* **Knopf, 1958.**
Moving and graphic story of the effects of a Nazi concentration camp on a small boy.

Downes, Donald. *The Easter dinner.* **Rinehart, 1960.**
An exciting and often humorous novel, set in Rome in 1944, and dealing with anti-fascist activities.

Downes, Donald. *Red rose for Maria.* **Rinehart, 1959.**
An exciting novel about espionage in Italy during the Second World War.

Elman, Richard M. *The 28th day of Elul.* **Scribner, 1967.**
Set in Hungary at the outbreak of World War II, this novel deals with the problems of Jews under Nazi persecution.

Elstob, Peter. *Warriors for the working day.* Coward, 1961.
About an English tank battalion in World War II, its training and its fighting.

Fielding, Gabriel. *The birthday king.* Morrow, 1963.
Excellent novel of a wealthy German family which is divided in its attitude toward Nazism and German war guilt.

Forbes, Colin. *Tramp in armor.* Dutton, 1970.
Exciting war story about a British tank and its crew, caught behind enemy lines in France in 1940, and how they made their way back to Dunkirk.

Forester, C. S. *The ship.* Little, 1943.
A masterly account of a British cruiser's battle in the Mediterranean in 1942.

Gainham, Sarah. *Night falls on the city.* Holt, 1967.
Long and dramatic story of Vienna under Nazi domination, and of an Austrian actress who struggles to hide her Jewish husband from the Gestapo.

Gainham, Sarah. *A place in the country.* Holt, 1969.
A sequel to *Night Falls on the City,* this deals with Vienna just after the Second World War, and the problems that beset people there.

Garth, David. *Watch on the bridge.* Putnam, 1959.
Tragic romance in the setting of the Allies' capture of Remagen bridge on the Rhine in 1945.

Geissler, Christian. *Sins of the fathers.* Random, 1962.
The Jewish purges in Nazi Germany, and their effect on the consciences of some Germans.

Gerlach, Heinrich. *Forsaken army.* Harper, 1959.
Powerful and vivid picture of the collapse of the German army at Stalingrad, written by one of its survivors.

Griffin, Gwyn. *An operational necessity.* **Putnam, 1967.**
Gripping story of the survivors of a freighter sunk by a U-boat in World War II, their ordeal in an open boat, and the capture and trial of the German officers of the sub. Realistic and dramatic.

Haedrich, Marcel. *The soldier and the rose.* **Putnam, 1962.**
A young Alsatian is imprisoned by the Germans in World War II; there are many sub-plots stressing the boredom and futility of war.

Hardy, Rene. *Bitter victory.* **Doubleday, 1956.**
A character study novel of two British Commandos at Benghazi in the Second World War.

Harris, Dale. *Home fires burning.* **Macmillan, 1968.**
About people in London during the blitz, and its effects on their habits and ways of thought.

Hartog, Jan de. *The captain.* **Atheneum, 1966.**
Story of Dutch ocean going tugs on the Murmansk run in the Second World War. Vivid realism and excitement.

Heinrich, Willi. *Crumbling fortress.* **Dial, 1963.**
Story of a group of refugees hiding in an abandoned building in the French Alps in 1944.

Herber, William. *Tomorrow to live.* **Coward, 1958.**
Novel about a company of Marines in the Saipan campaign of World War II.

Herisko, Ilona. *Brucknerstrasse.* **Messner, 1964.**
Story of three men in the waning days of Nazi glory, brought together among the lost ideals and pending tragedy of a German town.

Hersey, John. *The wall.* **Knopf, 1950.**
Long novel dealing with the Nazi extermination of the Jewish people of Warsaw.

Hutchinson, R. C. *Journey with strangers.* **Rinehart, 1952.**
A novel describing the tragic movement of a group of Polish refugees out of Poland, overrun by Nazis, and through Russia.

Hyams, Joseph. *Field of buttercups.* **Prentice, 1968.**
Deals movingly with the tragedy of the Jews of Warsaw under Nazi brutality.

Keefe, Frederick L. *The investigating officer.* **Dial, 1966.**
American officer in Vienna at the close of World War II is suspected of killing two SS men in cold blood.

Kelly, Michael. *Assault.* **Harcourt, 1968.**
Fast-paced and exciting story of attempt by British agents to destroy a German research center in Occupied Denmark.

Kernan, Thomas. *Now with the morning star.* **Scribner, 1944.**
Interesting and well-written book about a dedicated monk who, imprisoned in a monastery in the Black Forest, finds ways to fight the evils of Nazism.

Kirst, Hans H. *Forward, Gunner Asch.* **Little, 1956.**
Second volume of a trilogy about German troops in World War II. Stark and realistic picture of the common soldier in Russia and in a German base depot.

Kirst, Hans H. *Last stop Camp 7.* **Coward, 1969.**
Dramatic story of an American internment camp for former Nazis just after the war, during two intense days.

Kirst, Hans H. *Night of the generals.* **Harper, 1963.**
This is basically a detective story and a good one; but it is also a good historical and satirical novel about the German officer class during the Second World War.

Kirst, Hans H. *Return of Gunner Asch.* **Little, 1957.**
Last novel of the trilogy about the lot of a common soldier in the Nazi army.

99

Kirst, Hans H. *Revolt of Gunner Asch*. **Little, 1956.**
The first of three novels depicting realistically and satirically the life of a German soldier in the Second World War. This story is set in a German garrison town just before the outbreak of war.

Kirst, Hans H. *Soldiers' revolt*. **Harper, 1966.**
Story based on the plot to kill Hitler in July, 1944. Follows closely the actual history.

Kirst, Hans H. *The wolves*. **Coward, 1968.**
Powerful story of anti-Nazi underground in wartime Germany.

Klein-Haparash, J. *He who flees the lion*. **Atheneum, 1963.**
Novel about a wealthy Jewish family in Poland during World War II, and their struggle to avoid persecution.

Kluge, Alexander. *The battle*. **McGraw, 1967.**
Story of the Battle of Stalingrad in 1942, told by means of simulated documents and news bulletins.

Kuniczak, W. S. *The thousand hour day*. **Dial, 1966.**
Novel set in the period of the Nazi invasion of Poland in 1939, written by an eye-witness.

Kuznetsov, Anatoly. *Babi Yar*. **Dial, 1967.**
Nazi occupation of Kiev and massacres there in 1941-43. The author was there as a teen-ager and has thoroughly researched the events.

Landon, Christopher. *Flag in the city*. **Macmillan, 1954.**
Thriller of adventure and action in Persia during World War II. Good setting.

Langfus, Anna. *The whole land brimstone*. **Pantheon, 1962.**
Autobiographical novel of a young woman's escape from the Warsaw ghetto in 1939 and her efforts to survive throughout the war. Extreme realism.

Larteguy, Jean. *The centurions.* **Dutton, 1962.**
Gripping story about a small group of French colonial paratroop officers who fought in the loss of French Indo-China, suffered in a Communist POW camp, and then re-enlisted in the French forces in the rebellion in Algeria.

Larteguy, Jean. *The praetorians.* **Dutton, 1963.**
A sequel to *The Centurions,* carrying the same characters through the action and political intrigues of the Algerian revolution.

Levin, Meyer. *Eva.* **Simon & Schuster, 1959.**
Graphic story of a Jewish refugee girl in Nazi Germany, who is finally discovered and sent to Auschwitz. She escapes and eventually reaches Israel.

Levin, Meyer. *The stronghold.* **Simon & Schuster, 1965.**
Set near the end of World War II, this is the story of a refugee Nazi leader in a Bavarian castle, of an important Jewish hostage, and others of widely-differing points-of-view, with the inevitable conflicts.

Lucas, Ruth. *Who dare to live.* **Houghton, 1965.**
A young Englishwoman becomes involved in working for the anti-Nazi underground in Germany.

MacHardy, Charles. *Send down a dove.* **Coward, 1968.**
Highly authentic tale of submarine warfare in the British navy in World War II.

Mackiewicz, Jozef. *Road to nowhere.* **Regnery, 1964.**
Novel describing the conditions and conflicts of the Lithuanian occupation by the Soviets in 1940.

MacLean, Alistair. *Force 10 from Navarone.* **Doubleday, 1968.**
Another World War II high-voltage thriller by MacLean, set in the mountains of Yugoslavia.

101

MacLean, Alistair. *Guns of Navarone.* Doubleday, 1957.
A popular thriller of World War II. Not much history, but suspense in abundance.

MacLean, Alistair. *H.M.S. Ulysses.* Doubleday, 1956.
The author's first of several popular thrillers, this is a gripping story of a convoy vessel on the Murmansk run in World War II.

MacLean, Alistair. *Where eagles dare.* Doubleday, 1967.
Thrills, high adventure and almost unbearable suspense in this story of Allied agents infiltrating an enemy castle in the Alps in 1944.

Malcolm, Jean. *Discourse with shadows.* Doubleday, 1958.
A serious and somber novel on the brutalities of war, and especially of Nazi warfare.

Manning, Olivia. *Friends and heroes.* Doubleday, 1966.
Third novel of a trilogy about an English couple in the Balkans in the Second World War. Set in Athens.

Manning, Olivia. *The great fortune.* Doubleday, 1961.
An English professor in Bucharest and his bride await the German onslaught in 1940. Good picture of place and period.

Manning, Olivia. *The spoilt city.* Doubleday, 1962.
Rumanian aristocratic decadence at the outbreak of World War II, in the last days of King Carol.

Mazzeti, Lorenza. *The sky falls.* McKay, 1963.
Story about a Tuscan family in 1944 which has to cope with the many stresses of war. The narrator is a 10-year-old girl. Well-written.

Michener, James. *Bridges at Toko-ri.* Random, 1952.
Korean War story of a carrier bombing squadron assigned to cut enemy supply lines.

Mohrt, Michel. *The Italian campaign.* **Viking, 1967.**
Story of French Army officers on the Cote d'Azur just before and during the Second World War.

Monsey, Derek. *The hero.* **Knopf, 1961.**
Vivid and realistic account, largely autobiographical, of an English officer's escape from a Nazi prison and his difficult journey through Italy.

Montanelli, Indro. *General della Rovere.* **Doubleday, 1961.**
In Italy in 1944 the Germans employ an Italian swindler to impersonate a famous Italian general, which he does very successfully.

Moore, Brian. *The emperor of ice-cream.* **Viking, 1965.**
Story of a young and frustrated Irishman during World War II who gains the confidence he needs during the German bombing of Belfast.

Morganstern, Soma. *Third pillar.* **Farrar, 1955.**
A novel about the Nazi destruction of Polish Jews, symbolically written in biblical language.

Piper, David. *Trial by battle.* **Chilmark, 1965.**
A young Englishman's experiences in the Malayan defeat in World War II.

Plievier, Theodor. *Berlin.* **Doubleday, 1957.**
Describes vividly the downfall of the city in 1945.

Plievier, Theodor. *Moscow.* **Doubleday, 1954.**
Realistic novel about the German drive on Moscow in 1941.

Pontheir, Francois. *The fatal voyage.* **McKay, 1967.**
Story of naval action in World War II. Highly readable.

Powell, Anthony. *Valley of bones.* **Little, 1964.**
The seventh in Powell's series, "The Music of Time," this portrays British army life in a satiric fashion. Early part of World War II.

Ramati, Alexender. *Beyond the mountains.* **New Am. Lib., 1966.**
Written by a man who lived through similar experiences, this is the story of two Polish brothers in Siberia during the German invasion of 1941 who try to reach the Free Polish forces.

Rasmussen, Gerhard. *No leave for the captain.* **Crowell, 1958.**
Gripping short novel about two men in the British Naval Mine Disposal Corps who, during World War Two, are assigned to deactivate two unusual German mines.

Rayner, Denys. *Enemy below.* **Holt, 1956.**
Exciting story of a "duel" between a German submarine and an English destroyer in World War II, written by a former English destroyer officer.

Reeman, Douglas. *The pride and the anguish.* **Putnam, 1969.**
The fall of Singapore in 1941, as seen by a British naval officer. Authentic setting, much action and suspense.

Remarque, Erich. *Night in Lisbon.* **Harcourt, 1964.**
The story of a man and his wife, refugees in 1942, who escape from Germany to Paris and eventually through France to Lisbon.

Robinson, Wayne. *Barbara.* **Doubleday, 1961.**
An authentic story of tank warfare in the Second World War.

Ross, James E. *The dead are mine.* **McKay, 1963.**
Realistic story of the fighting on the Anzio beachhead in 1944, as seen by an American sergeant.

Roth, Arthur. *A terrible beauty.* **Farrar, 1958.**
Story of the I.R.A. in Ulster during the Second World War, when anti-British feeling was very high.

Sahl, Hans. *The few and the many.* **Harcourt, 1962.**
Novel about exiles from Hitler's Germany, enduring homelessness and frustration in their wanderings.

St. John, Robert. *Man who played God.* **Doubleday, 1962.**
Story of a man who, during the Nazi persecution of Jews in Hungary,
tried to buy the freedom of thousands of them.

Scott, Paul. *Mark of the warrior.* **Morrow, 1958.**
A good novel dealing with the problems of a group of Englishmen
training for jungle warfare in Burma.

Sentjurc, Igor. *The torrents of war.* **McKay, 1962.**
The German army in the Russian campaign in World War II; realistic and vivid.

Silberstang, Edwin. *Nightmare of the dark.* **Knopf, 1967.**
Story of a boy and his mother who are captives in Dachau during the
Second World War. Very realistic.

Thompson, A. L. B. *A battle is fought to be won.* **Coward, 1961.**
About a British officer commanding a detachment of Burmese
soldiers in a losing fight against the on-moving Japanese.

Tobino, Mario. *The underground.* **Doubleday, 1964.**
The organizing of an underground resistance to German occupation
in an Italian town after the fall of Mussolini.

Trevor, Elleston. *Big pick-up.* **Macmillan, 1955.**
Highly graphic and action-packed novel of one group of British
soldiers who make their way to Dunkirk and home.

Trevor, Elleston. *Killing-ground.* **Macmillan, 1957.**
Good realistic writing about a small British tank troop in the
Normandy invasion.

Tute, Warren. *The rock.* **Sloane, 1959.**
A World War II novel, set in and around Gibraltar, with intricate
personal conflicts and vivid sea action.

Uris, Leon. *Angry hills.* Random, 1955.
Exciting espionage story in Greece during the German invasion.

Uris, Leon. *Exodus.* Doubleday, 1958.
Long and detailed novel covering the whole story of the formation of the State of Israel.

Wagner, Geoffrey. *The sands of valor.* Knopf, 1967.
A British tank regiment fighting in North Africa against Rommel provides the characters and action for this novel.

Waugh, Evelyn. *Men at arms.* Little, 1952.
A witty and sardonic picture of the British Army in 1939, as seen by an Englishman who enlisted.

Waugh, Evelyn. *Officers and gentlemen.* Little, 1955.
Sequel to *Men at Arms,* this continues the satirical adventures of a gentleman volunteer in the British forces in World War II.

Wescott, Glenway. *Apartment in Athens.* Harper, 1945.
Excellent novel of the Nazi occupation of Greece, in which a German officer bullies and nearly destroys a Greek family with whom he is quartered.

Westheimer, David. *Song of the young sentry.* Little, 1968.
Experiences in a series of World War II prisoner-of-war camps make a man of a previously weak, self-pitying aviator. Settings are vivid and realistic.

Westheimer, David. *Von Ryan's express.* Doubleday, 1963.
A genuine thriller, subsequently made into a movie, of a tough American officer in an Italian POW camp, and how he freed the whole group during a Nazi attempt to move them to Germany.

White, Theodore. *Mountain road.* Sloane, 1958.
Story of American forces in Asia during World War II. Written by an expert on China.

Zarubica, Mladin. *Year of the rat.* Harcourt, 1964.
An espionage thriller of World War II, purportedly based on real events, including the disappearance of Nazi Martin Bormann.

Zeno. *The cauldron.* Stein & Day, 1967.
Story about the Allied attempt to capture German-held Arnheim in the Netherlands in 1944.

JUVENILE

Armstrong, Richard. *Fight for freedom.* McKay, 1966.
Young British seaman is involved in fighting in Crete during World War II.

Armstrong, Richard. *Ship afire!* Day, 1960.
Exciting story of a torpedoed British oil tanker en route from Halifax to Britain in World War II.

Benary-Isbert, Margot. *The ark.* Harcourt, 1953.
Problems of a West German refugee family after World War II.

Benary-Isbert, Margot. *Dangerous spring.* Harcourt, 1961.
About a German doctor's family in the last years of World War II as the country collapses. For teen-age girls.

Benary-Isbert, Margot. *A time to love.* Harcourt, 1962.
Story of a girl at boarding school in Germany during the rise of Nazism, and the problems she faces because of anti-Jewish persecution.

Bishop, Claire. *Twenty and ten.* Viking, 1952.
World War II story of 20 French children cared for in the mountains by a nun, and of how they aided ten Jewish children to escape the Nazis.

Forman, James. *Ring the Judas bell.* **Farrar, 1965.**
A group of children escaping from Greek communists after World War Two, learn the meaning of courage and patriotism in the wild hills. Excellent story.

Forman, James. *Skies of Crete.* **Farrar, 1963.**
Two young people and their grandfather are involved in the defence of Crete against Nazi invasion in 1941.

Hilton, Irene. *Enemy in the sky.* **Westminster, 1964.**
About two children's experiences after their mother is killed in the Nazi blitz of London in 1944.

Hunt, Mabel. *Singing among strangers.* **Lippincott, 1954.**
A girl's story about a Latvian family in World War II who finally emigrated to America.

Levin, Jane W. *Star of danger.* **Harcourt, 1966.**
Story of two Jewish boys in Denmark during the Second World War, and how they were aided to escape the Nazis.

McKown, Robin. *Patriot of the underground.* **Putnam, 1964.**
Adventure story about a group of boys who become anti-Nazi saboteurs in occupied France during the war.

Senje, Sigurd. *Escape!* **Harcourt, 1964.**
About the activities of two young members of the Norwegian underground in World War II, who aid a friend to escape the Nazis.

Serraillier, Ian. *Silver sword.* **Criterion, 1959.**
Vivid story about how three Polish children manage to survive in Nazi-occupied Warsaw after their parents are killed.

Seth, Ronald. *Spy and the atom gun.* **Farrar, 1958.**
Tense and exciting story of a British agent operating back of the Iron Curtain.

Seymour, Alta. *Toward morning.* **Follett, 1961.**
A group of young Hungarian patriots fighting to obtain freedom
from Russian control in the 1956 uprising.

Sommerfelt, Aimee. *Miriam.* **Criterion, 1963.**
About a Jewish family in Nazi-occupied Norway.

Stiles, Martha. *Darkness over the land.* **Dial, 1966.**
Story of life in Nazi Germany under Gestapo terror. Excellent
picture of a time of fear and courage.

Tunis, John. *Silence over Dunkerque.* **Morrow, 1962.**
Story of two British boys and their father, involved in the great effort
to evacuate British forces.

Werstein, Irving. *The long escape.* **Scribner, 1964.**
Story of the escape of a group of children from Nazi control through
Dunkirk to England.

ASIA, AFRICA AND THE PACIFIC

ASIA

Andrews, Laurie. *Deadly patrol.* **McKay, 1957.**
Vivid depiction of jungle warfare in Burma during World War II.

Augur, Helen. *Tall ships to Cathay.* **Doubleday, 1951.**
Romance, adventure and the Far East in a story of the clipper trade with China in the early 19th century. Good research.

Boulle, Pierre. *Bridge over the River Kwai.* **Vanguard, 1954.**
One of the most distinguished of World War II novels, later made into an equally fine motion picture. An exciting novel of drama and psychological suspense.

Bourne, Peter. *Twilight of the dragon.* **Putnam, 1954.**
Story of the Boxer Rebellion, with good portrayal of the Dowager Empress.

Bridge, Ann. *The dark moment.* **Macmillan, 1951.**
Good novel depicting Turkey during and after World War I, as it started to become westernized.

Buck, Pearl. *Imperial woman.* **Day, 1955.**
Memorable portrait of Tzu-hsi, the last Empress of China and a remarkable woman.

Buck, Pearl. *The living reed.* **Day, 1963.**
A history of Korea from 1881 to 1952, told as the story of a powerful family through four generations.

Butler, William. *The ring in Meiji.* **Putnam, 1965.**
Long novel with a wide range of characters, action and pageantry. Set in 19th century Japan as it begins to emerge into the western orbit of influence.

Chavchavadze, Paul. *Mountains of Allah.* **Doubleday, 1952.**
Story of adventure set in the Caucasus in the 1850's during fighting between Russians and Turks.

Clavell, James. *Tai-pan.* **Atheneum, 1966.**
Long, well-told story of the efforts of an English merchant in China
in the 1840's to gain control of Hong Kong for England.

Cleary, Jon. *The long pursuit.* **Morrow, 1967.**
Set in Sumatra in 1942, it is the gripping story of civilians left behind
by the swift passage of war, and forced to shift for themselves.

Clift, Charmian and Johnston, George. *Big chariot.* **Bobbs, 1953.**
The setting is 17th century China, with vivid accounts of brotherly
rivalry and local warfare.

Clou, John. *Caravan to Camul.* **Bobbs, 1954.**
Well-researched novel dealing with the early years of Genghis Khan.

Costain, Thomas B. *Black rose.* **Doubleday, 1945.**
Colorful and exciting story of a 13th century Englishman who travels
to the Far East and finds romance and adventure there.

Duggan, Alfred. *Knight with armour.* **Coward, 1951.**
The story of an Englishman's pilgrimage to the Holy Land around
1100, told with authentic background detail.

Duggan, Alfred. *Lady for ransom.* **Coward, 1953.**
Fine historical novel of the 11th century in Byzantium, with authentic
and colorful settings and action.

Gardner, Mona. *Hong Kong.* **Doubleday, 1958.**
Romance and adventure in the setting of the Chinese Opium Wars
and the establishment of Hong Kong as a British colony.

Graves, Robert. *Count Belisarius.* **Random, 1938.**
Long and impressive novel of the Byzantine Empire in the sixth
century, dealing with Belisarius, the general, and the Emperor
Justinian.

111

Groseclose, Elgin. *The Carmelite.* **Macmillan, 1955.**
Good unusual setting in this novel about a missionary sent to 17th
century Persia. The action is engrossing and the background
authentic.

Harris, John. *Jade wind.* **Doubleday, 1969.**
About some young American flyers who, in 1926, went to China to
train pilots for a warlord and became involved in a civil war.

John, Evan. *Ride home tomorrow.* **Putnam, 1951.**
Enjoyable novel set in the Christian Kingdom of Jerusalem in the
12th century.

Kaye, Mary M. *Shadow of the moon.* **Messner, 1957.**
Authentic picture of 19th century India, set in the events of the
Sepoy Rebellion of 1857.

Kossak-Szczucka, Zofja. *The leper king.* **Roy, 1945.**
Colorful novel about the last years of the Christian Kingdom of
Jerusalem in the time of Baldwin IV.

Lampard, David. *Present from Peking.* **Doubleday, 1965.**
Set in China in 1947-48 during the Communist Revolution, a story
of a British flyer who becomes involved on the Nationalist side.

Lancaster, Bruce. *Venture in the East.* **Little, 1951.**
A story about members of the Dutch East India Company as they
lived and traded in Japan in the early 1600's. Good picture of
medieval Japan.

Lewis, Mildred. *Honorable sword.* **Houghton, 1960.**
A story of two boys' adventures during a siege of a castle in medieval
Japan.

Li, Chin-Yang. *Madame Goldenflower.* **Farrar, 1960.**
About the Boxer Rebellion in Peking in 1900. Good authentic
background.

Lund, Robert. *Daishi-san.* **Day, 1961.**
Novel about William Adams, an Elizabethan shipmaster who became the first Englishman in Japan.

Masefield, John. *Basilissa.* **Macmillan, 1940.**
A novel about Byzantium and the Empress Theodora, whom the poet makes appear better than her reputation.

Masefield, John. *Conquer.* **Macmillan, 1941.**
Excellent brief novel of an exciting episode in 6th century Byzantium.

Masters, John. *Coromandel!* **Viking, 1955.**
Action-packed story of an Englishman's adventures in early 17th century India.

Masters, John. *The deceivers.* **Viking, 1952.**
Novel of India in the 19th century, by a specialist in the Indian setting. Very realistic in dealing with the cult which produced the thugs, professional assassins.

Masters, John. *Nightrunners of Bengal.* **Viking, 1950.**
Exciting, vivid and highly authentic fictional account of the Sepoy Rebellion of 1857.

McKenna, Richard. *The Sand Pebbles.* **Harper, 1962.**
Full of action and realism, this is the story of an American patrol boat plying Chinese rivers in the 1920's, prior to the outbreak of revolution.

Meacham, Ellis K. *The East Indiaman.* **Little, 1968.**
Well told in the tradition of C. S. Forester, these adventures of an 18th century naval captain are set in the Far East.

Michener, James. *Caravans.* **Random, 1963.**
This novel is set in the exotic and remote kingdom of Afghanistan in 1946, and tells of the search for a young American girl who has been missing there for a year.

Monsarrat, Nicholas. *The white rajah.* **Sloane, 1961.**
Picaresque novel about an Englishman who turns pirate in the East Indies, befriends a rajah and finally takes his place. Much action and glamor.

O'Connor, Richard. *The Vandal.* **Doubleday, 1960.**
Story of a soldier in the Byzantine army under Belisarius in the 5th century, and the campaign against invading Persians.

O'Neal, Cothburn. *Master of the world.* **Crown, 1952.**
A lusty and violent story of the Mongol conqueror, Tamerlane.

Payne, Robert. *Young emperor.* **Macmillan, 1950.**
Set in 17th century India. Historical romance.

Raja, Rao. *Kanthapura.* **New Directions, 1963.**
Pictures Gandhi's efforts to gain freedom from British rule as they appeared in one small Indian village.

Scarfoglio, Carlo. *True Cross.* **Pantheon, 1955.**
About the Latin Kingdom in Palestine during the later period of the Second Crusade (1177-1192).

Schoonover, Lawrence. *Gentle infidel.* **Macmillan, 1950.**
Fast-moving adventure in Turkey around 1450, as a Christian orphan is raised to be a Moslem janizary.

Shelby, Graham. *Knights of dark renown.* **Weybright & Talley, 1970.**
Vivid picture of Jerusalem around 1183, as the European control is drawing to a close under the pressure of the Moslems.

Thomson, Stewart. *Show of force.* **Harper, 1955.**
International intrigue and danger involving, in the period between the wars, British resident oilmen in an Arabian oil area.

Waltari, Mika. *Dark angel.* **Putnam, 1952.**
The scene is Constantinople in the year of its downfall to the Turks. Battles, romance and color.

Wellman, Paul. *The female.* **Doubleday, 1953.**
Novel about Theodora, the courtesan who became the wife of Justinian and Empress of the Byzantine Empire. Long and melodramatic.

Wolpert, Stanley. *Nine hours to Rama.* **Random, 1962.**
Fictionalized study of the assassin of Mahatma Gandhi, and of the background that produced the murder.

JUVENILE

Bartos-Hoppner, B. *Save the Khan.* **Walck, 1964.**
Story of a Tartar prince in the 16th century fighting against Russian invaders of Siberia. Exciting and well-written.

Baumann, Hans. *Sons of the steppe.* **Oxford U. P., 1958.**
Good story of two grandsons of Genghis Khan, who receive the same warlike training but react to it in different ways.

Bothwell, Jean. *Omen for a princess.* **Abelard, 1963.**
About the daughter of the Indian emperor who built the Taj Mahal.

Bothwell, Jean. *Promise of the rose.* **Harcourt, 1958.**
Romance and mystery story for girls, set in 16th century India with authentic background.

Bruckner, Karl. *The day of the bomb.* **Van Nostrand, 1963.**
Twelve vivid descriptions of the tragedy of Hiroshima.

Daringer, Helen. *Flower of Araby.* **Harcourt, 1958.**
Story for girls about the daughter of an English knight in 13th century Syria. Unusual setting.

De Jong, Meindert. *The house of sixty fathers.* **Harper, 1956.**
Adventure and excitement in this story about a Chinese family scattered by a Japanese invasion before the War.

Donauer, Friedrich. *Long defence.* **Longmans, 1931.**
Exciting and graphic story of a boy in the siege and fall of Constantinople in 1453.

Dubois, Theodora. *Tiger burning bright.* **Farrar, 1963.**
Young English girl in India during the Sepoy Rebellion leads a group of small children out of Delhi to safety.

Fon Eisen, Anthony. *Prince of Omeya.* **World, 1964.**
Gripping adventure story set in 8th century Islam.

Hollister, Mary. *Pagoda anchorage.* **Dodd, 1939.**
Story of adventure and romance for girls, set in Fukien, China, in the days of the clipper trade.

Honour, Alan. *Cave of riches.* **McGraw, 1956.**
The story of how a Bedouin boy found the famous Dead Sea Scrolls.

Lamb, Harold. *Chief of the Cossacks.* **Random, 1959.**
A stirring account of the legendary 17th century Cossack leader, Stenka Razin. Good authentic settings.

Polland, Madeleine. *Mission to Cathay.* **Doubleday, 1965.**
Story based on the efforts of a priest to establish the first Catholic mission in 16th century China.

Ritchie, Rita. *Golden hawks of Genghis Khan.* **Dutton, 1958.**
Unusual background about hawking in 13th century Asia.

Ritchie, Rita. *Year of the horse.* **Dutton, 1957.**
About a boy's exciting life among the Mongols of Genghis Khan.

Sandoz, Edouard. *Twice besieged.* **Oxford U. P., 1947.**
Boy's adventures fighting with the Crusaders at the siege of Antioch in the 11th century.

Stinetorf, Louise. *The shepherd of Abu Kush.* **Day, 1962.**
Involves problems of Arab evacuation in the new state of Israel.

Treece, Henry. *The golden one.* **Criterion, 1962.**
Two young people involved in the complicated struggles among the
Knights Templars, the Tartars, and the Assassins finally reach the
court of Genghis Khan.

Treece, Henry. *Swords from the north.* **Pantheon, 1967.**
Tale of a viking, Harold the Stern, as a warrior at the Byzantine
court.

Welch, Ronald. *Knight crusader.* **Oxford U. P., 1955.**
Adventures of a youth who grew up in a crusader's castle in the
Holy Land in the 12th century, and fought in the Second Crusade.

AFRICA

Abrahams, Peter. *Wild conquest.* **Harper, 1950.**
A vigorous story of the Great Trek of the Boers in the 1830's.

Achebe, Chinua. *Things fall apart.* **Obolensky, 1959.**
Written by a Nigerian, this is an excellent picture of village life
there in the late 19th century, and of one man in particular whose
values and beliefs are shattered by the coming of white men.

Aldridge, James. *The last exile.* **Doubleday, 1961.**
Very long but well-told story of people involved in the troubles in
Egypt at the time of the Suez Canal take-over by Nasser.

Cloete, Stuart. *The fiercest heart.* **Houghton, 1960.**
The Boer trek in South Africa in the 1830's.

Cloete, Stuart. *Rags of glory.* **Doubleday, 1963.**
Action-filled and engrossing novel of the Boer War, with Smuts,
Rhodes, Kitchener, Kruger and other great names.

Cloete, Stuart. *The turning wheels.* **Houghton, 1937.**
Excellent portrayal of the Great Trek of the Boers in 1836 from the
English Cape Colony to the new lands of Transvaal.

Cloete, Stuart. *Watch for the dawn.* **Houghton, 1939.**
Good novel of a young Boer farmer in South Africa in 1816, and of
the tragedy of the Boer-English conflict.

Gartner, Chloe. *Drums of Khartoum.* **Morrow, 1967.**
The setting is the siege and capture of Khartoum by the Mahdi in
1885. Romance and action.

Knight, Brigid. *Covenant.* **Crowell, 1943.**
About an English family living in South Africa at the time of the
Boer War. Good background.

Krepps, Robert. *Earthshaker.* **Macmillan, 1958.**
Adventure and fortune-hunting in primitive South Africa in the
late 1800's.

Montupet, Jeanne. *Red fountain.* **St. Martins, 1961.**
Story of three generations of a French family in Algeria, involved in
the struggle for Algerian independence.

Rooke, Daphne. *Wizard's country.* **Houghton, 1957.**
Well-written story of a Zulu tribe fighting against the English in
1870.

Scholefield, Alan. *Eagles of malice.* **Morrow, 1968.**
Adventure story in German South West Africa around 1905. Bitter
warfare between natives and Germans.

Scholefield, Alan. *Great elephant.* **Morrow, 1968.**
Story about the first white family to settle in Zululand in the early
19th century. Good adventure tale.

Slaughter, Frank G. *Deadly lady of Madagascar.* **Doubleday, 1959.**
Piracy, romance and action in the Indian Ocean in the early 18th century.

Steinhouse, Herbert. *Time of the Juggernaut.* **Morrow, 1958.**
The story of an American newspaperman in France who, in 1955, becomes closely involved in the Algerian problem.

Trevor, Elleston. *The freebooters.* **Doubleday, 1967.**
Adventure story of terrorism and desert fighting in East Africa. Much action and atmosphere.

Van der Post, Laurens. *The hunter and the whale.* **Morrow, 1967.**
Whaling off the coasts of South Africa around 1920, with a plot reminiscent of *Moby Dick.*

Young, Francis B. *They seek a country.* **Reynal, 1937.**
Powerful novel of an English convict's voyage on a prison ship to South Africa in the 1830's, his escape and his experiences among the Boers at the time of the Great Trek.

JUVENILE

Maddock, Reginald. *Last horizon.* **Nelson, 1962.**
A powerful story of the futile effort of the African Bushmen to hold their land against the advancing Boer settlers.

Wibberley, Leonard. *Secret of the hawk.* **Ariel, 1953.**
Story of an 18th century English boy who goes to Africa and finds his uncle engaged in slave trading.

AUSTRALIA AND THE PACIFIC

Blunden, Godfrey. *Charco Harbour.* **Vanguard, 1968.**
Lusty adventure story of Captain James Cook's discovery of Australia.

119

Boyd, Martin. *Outbreak of love.* **Reynal, 1957.**
A romantic comedy of manners about an upper-class family in Melbourne in the early 20th century.

Bushnell, O. A. *Molokai.* **World, 1963.**
A moving and inspiring novel about the work of Father Damien, the priest who served a leper colony in Hawaii in the mid-19th century.

Bushnell, O. A. *Return of Lono.* **Little, 1956.**
Novel about Captain Cook's last voyage to the South Pacific and his tragic death in Hawaii.

Close, Robert. *Eliza Callaghan.* **Doubleday, 1957.**
Story of a London girl who is sent to Australia as a convict and finds romance in the early days there.

Dark, Eleanor. *Storm of time.* **McGraw, 1950.**
Interesting novel about a wide variety of the people in Australia in the early 1800's. Setting and characterizations very well done.

Dark, Eleanor. *The timeless land.* **Macmillan, 1941.**
A well-written novel about the earliest white settlers in Australia, and about the reaction of the aborigines toward them.

Dick, Isabel. *Wild orchard.* **Crowell, 1945.**
Story of a young Englishwoman who, in 1840, marries a visiting landowner from Tasmania and returns there with him to pioneer the land.

Eden, Dorothy. *Sleep in the woods.* **Coward, 1961.**
Romance about a group of English girls who go to 19th century New Zealand to find homes and husbands among the pioneers.

Gaskin, Catherine. *I know my love.* **Doubleday, 1962.**
Romance set in the gold rush and pioneer conditions of Australia in the 1850's.

Gaskin, Catherine. *Sara Dane.* **Lippincott, 1955.**
Based partly on fact, this is the story of a young woman convict
sent from England to Australia in 1792, who marries a ship's officer
and eventually rises to wealth and prominence in the new country.

Graves, Robert. *Islands of unwisdom.* **Doubleday, 1949.**
Novel based on a Spanish expedition in 1595 which attempted to
establish a colony in the Solomon Islands.

Lancaster, G. B. *Promenade.* **Reynal, 1938.**
Colorful and authentic account of the settlement of New Zealand
during the 19th century.

Lofts, Norah. *Silver nutmeg.* **Doubleday, 1947.**
Story about a wealthy Dutch merchant and his wife in the East Indies
in 1656, involved in a native uprising.

Mason, Van Wyck. *Harpoon in Eden.* **Doubleday, 1969.**
A lusty tale of a Nantucket whaling voyage to New Zealand in the
1830's.

Mason, Van Wyck. *Manila galleon.* **Little, 1960.**
Long and adventure-filled story of Commodore Anson's squadron
in the Pacific in 1740.

McGinnis, Paul. *Lost Eden.* **McBride, 1947.**
Adventures of an 18th century Englishman who sails to the South
Seas with Cook and settles in the Hawaiian Islands.

Michener, James. *Hawaii.* **Random, 1959.**
Very long and engrossing novel involving all the separate streams
of people who made up the early settlement of Hawaii.

Nordhoff, Charles and Hall, James. *Botany Bay.* **Little, 1941.**
Graphic picture of life in the Australian penal colony in the late 18th
century.

Nordhoff, Charles and Hall, James. *Bounty Trilogy.* **Little, 1936.**
A one-volume edition of the classic novels, *Mutiny on the Bounty,
Men Against the Sea,* and *Pitcairn's Island,* which together form the
story of the ship, its master, and the mutineers.

Teilhet, Darwin. *Mission of Jeffery Tolamy.* **Sloane, 1951.**
Set in Hawaii in the early 1800's, this is a story of Russian efforts
to take over the islands.

Wilson, Erle. *Adams of the "Bounty".* **Criterion, 1959.**
John Adams was one of the *Bounty* mutineers and a leader on Pitcairn Island. This novel makes him the central figure and gives a
different aspect of the whole affair from that of Nordhoff and Hall.

JUVENILE

Hewes, Agnes. *With the will to go.* **Longmans, 1960.**
A 16th century seafaring adventure story of how the Dutch out-
stripped the Spanish and Portuguese in the competition for the
Indies trade.

Knight, Frank. *Golden monkey.* **St. Martins, 1953.**
Story of an English boy's adventures on a British sailing ship around
1860, going to Australia and back.

Locke, Elsie. *Runaway settlers.* **Dutton, 1966.**
An Australian woman and her six children leave home to make a new
life as pioneers in primitive New Zealand in 1860.

Sperry, Armstrong. *Danger to windward.* **Winston, 1947.**
Story of a boy's experiences on a whaling voyage to the South
Pacific in the early 19th century.

Thum, Marcella. *Anne of the Sandwich Islands.* **Dodd, 1967.**
About the experiences of a young American girl who accompanied
a missionary group to the Sandwich Islands in 1840, hoping to find
her father who had disappeared there.

THE UNITED STATES

DISCOVERY AND EXPLORATION

Brady, Charles A. *This land fulfilled.* **Dutton, 1958.**
Story of Leif Ericsson's historic voyage to Vinland. Colorful
re-creation.

Fletcher, Inglis. *Roanoke hundred.* **Bobbs, 1948.**
Novel of exciting action about the Grenville expedition to Virginia
in the 16th century, and the battle off the Azores in which Grenville
was killed.

Forester, C. S. *To the Indies.* **Little, 1940.**
Fine novel about Columbus's third voyage, from which he returned
in chains. Good action and impressive pictures of the new world.

Fuller, Iola. *The gilded torch.* **Putnam, 1957.**
Good story about twin brothers from France who accompanied
La Salle in his American explorations.

Hersch, Virginia. *Seven cities of gold.* **Duell, 1946.**
Colorful novel of Coronado's epic journey from Mexico to what is
now Kansas — the first white man to see that vast middle America.

Jennings, John. *Golden eagle.* **Putnam, 1959.**
Fictionalized account of the adventurous career of Hernando de Soto.

Lytle, Andrew. *At the Moon's Inn.* **Bobbs, 1941.**
Tale of adventure based on the explorations of Hernando De Soto.

Maass, Edgar. *Don Pedro and the devil.* **Bobbs, 1942.**
Colorful story of a young Spaniard who goes with Pizarro to Peru,
hoping to gain a fortune and the hand of the girl he left behind him.

Salverson, Laura. *Immortal rock.* **Bouregy, 1954.**
Good novel dealing with the 14th century Norse expedition to
America, and the Kensington Stone.

Shellabarger, Samuel. *Captain from Castile.* **Little, 1944.**
Cloak-and-dagger romance and adventure which moves colorfully
between Spain and Mexico in the 1500's.

Spence, Hartzell. *Vain shadow.* **McGraw, 1947.**
A good fictionalized biography of Orellana, who discovered the
Amazon River.

Tebbel, John. *Touched with fire.* **Dutton, 1952.**
La Salle's career as an explorer in early America is the basis for this
novel.

Tracy, Don. *Roanoke renegade.* **Dial, 1954.**
Novel involving a speculation of what happened to the lost colony
sent out by Raleigh.

JUVENILE

Allen, Merritt P. *Wilderness way.* **Longmans, 1954.**
Story of a French boy who comes to New France and joins La Salle's
expedition down the Mississippi.

Baumann, Hans. *Son of Columbus.* **Oxford U. P., 1957.**
Story about Columbus' fourth voyage to the New World, as his
younger son may have seen it.

Engle, Eloise. *Sea challenge.* **Hammond, 1962.**
Two boys accompany Magellan on his epic voyage of discovery.

Haig-Brown, Roderick. *Whale people.* **Morrow, 1963.**
A story of primitive pre-Columbian Indians of the Pacific Northwest,
who lived mainly by hunting whales.

Kjelgaard, James. *Buckskin brigade.* **Holiday, 1947.**
Told in fictional form, this is a series of accounts of the exploration of
North America over a three-century period.

Lobdell, Helen. *King's snare.* Houghton, 1955.
Adventure on Raleigh's voyage of exploration up the Orinoco River.

Merrill, Leigh. *Tenoch.* Nelson, 1954.
About early California when the first Spanish explorers came there.

Paxton, S. H. *Dragon in New Albion.* Little, 1953.
Boys' story of Drake's visit to the coast of California in the 1570's.

Powers, Alfred. *Chains for Columbus.* Westminster, 1948.
A boy becomes a follower of Columbus when he is imprisoned after his third voyage, and accompanies him on his fourth.

Resnick, William S. *Dragonship.* Coward, 1942.
Story of a boy in an early Norse settlement in America.

THE COLONIAL PERIOD

Alderman, Clifford. *Silver keys.* Putnam, 1960.
Story of adventure in the late 17th century, mainly about Sir William Phips' expedition from New England to the Caribbean to raise sunken Spanish treasure.

Alderman, Clifford. *To fame unknown.* Appleton, 1954.
Romantic adventure set during the later years of the French and Indian Wars.

Allen, Hervey. *Bedford Village.* Farrar, 1944.
The second in Allen's series of frontier and Indian life in western Pennsylvania in the 1760's.

Allen, Hervey. *Forest and the fort.* Farrar, 1943.
First volume of Allen's outstanding series of novels on the frontier of western Pennsylvania during the French and Indian War.

Allen, Hervey. *Toward the morning.* **Rinehart, 1948.**
This is the third in Allen's fine series on the life of the frontier; here his hero, Salathiel Albine, prepares to come east to Philadelphia during the 1760's.

Bacheller, Irving. *Candle in the wilderness.* **Bobbs, 1930.**
Boston in the days of Puritan supremacy.

Barker, Shirley. *Peace, my daughters.* **Crown, 1949.**
Story of the witchcraft hysteria in colonial Salem.

Barker, Shirley. *Rivers parting.* **Crown, 1950.**
Novel whose settings include 17th century New Hampshire and London. Good background of New England colonial period.

Barker, Shirley. *Tomorrow the new moon.* **Bobbs, 1955.**
Very good picture of village life on Martha's Vineyard in colonial times, centering around three English newcomers.

Borland, Barbara. *The greater hunger.* **Appleton, 1962.**
Set in the early New England of the first settlers, it is a story of romance, intolerance and men against nature.

Breslin, Howard. *Bright battalions.* **McGraw, 1952.**
Story about an Irishman serving with the French forces in northern New York during the French and Indian War. Exciting action plus romance.

Cannon, Legrand. *Come home at even.* **Holt, 1951.**
A story of religious troubles in England and New England, with Roger Williams a principal character.

Cannon, Legrand. *Look to the mountain.* **Holt, 1942.**
Long but vivid and engrossing story of a young couple who settled in the New Hampshire wilderness just before the Revolution.

Chidsey, Donald B. *Captain Adam.* **Crown, 1953.**
An adventure story of piracy, smuggling and other bits of derring-do
off the American coast in the early 18th century.

Crabb, Alfred L. *Journey to Nashville.* **Bobbs, 1957.**
A story of the pioneers who, coming from the Watauga settlements
in East Tennessee, first settled Nashville.

Curwood, James. *Plains of Abraham.* **Doubleday, 1928.**
A novel of the French and Indian War.

Dodge, Constance. *In Adam's fall.* **Macrae Smith, 1946.**
A story of the Salem witchcraft craze.

Dowdey, Clifford. *Gamble's hundred.* **Little, 1939.**
The great plantations and people of colonial Virginia in the early
18th century.

Du Bois, Theodora. *Freedom's way.* **Funk, 1953.**
Story of an English girl sent to America as an indentured servant
shortly before the Revolution.

Edmonds, Walter D. *In the hands of the Senecas.* **Little, 1947.**
A well-written story of New York pioneer life in the 1770's, when
Indians were the terrible enemy. Authentic and graphic.

Ethridge, Willie. *Summer thunder.* **Coward, 1958.**
Romance in the setting of the founding of the Georgia colony by
Oglethorpe in the 1730's.

Flannagan, Roy. *Forest cavalier.* **Bobbs, 1952.**
A story of Bacon's Rebellion in colonial Virginia, especially good
in historical details.

Fletcher, Inglis. *Cormorant's brood.* **Lippincott, 1959.**
North Carolina in the 1720's, when a greedy British governor arouses
the anger of the people.

Fletcher, Inglis. *Lusty wind for Carolina.* **Bobbs, 1944.**
Authentic story about Huguenot settlers on the Cape Fear River of
North Carolina in the early 18th century.

Fletcher, Inglis. *Wind in the forest.* **Bobbs, 1957.**
Story dealing with the conflicts between frontier farmers and coastal
planters in North Carolina before the Revolution.

Gay, Margaret. *Hatchet in the sky.* **Simon & Schuster, 1954.**
The French and Indian War and Pontiac's Conspiracy around the
frontier outpost, Detroit.

Gebler, Ernest. *Plymouth adventure.* **Doubleday, 1950.**
Realistic and well-researched novel about the voyage of the
Mayflower and the first Plymouth winter.

Gerson, Noel. *The highwayman.* **Doubleday, 1955.**
Adventure and excitement in the French-English struggles in
America before the Revolution.

Gerson, Noel. *Imposter.* **Doubleday, 1954.**
Romance and swashbuckling adventure in Port Royal at the time of
the 1692 earthquake.

Gerson, Noel. *King's Messenger.* **Farrar, 1956.**
Light and active tale of adventure in the colonies before the
Revolution, as the hero works for the British against the French.

Gerson, Noel. *Savage gentleman.* **Doubleday, 1950.**
About a group of people in the Mohawk Valley during Queen Anne's
War in the early 1700's.

Giles, Janice. *Hannah Fowler.* **Houghton, 1956.**
Well-written novel about pioneer conditions in Kentucky at the time
of the Revolution.

Golon, Sergeanne. *Countess Angelique.* **Putnam, 1968.**
This is the sixth in a series of excellent tales about Angelique. It is
set in the wilds of 17th century Maine and provides fine adventure.

Hamilton, Harry. *Thunder in the wilderness.* **Bobbs, 1949.**
An action story of French and Indians in the Mississippi valley
around 1760.

Jennings, John. *Gentleman ranker.* **Reynal, 1942.**
A young English wastrel finds himself in Virginia as a foot soldier
in Braddock's army in the French and Indian War.

Jennings, John. *Next to valour.* **Macmillan, 1939.**
An over-long but exciting adventure story and romance about a
young Scotsman who came to New Hampshire in 1745 and took
part in Indian fights and the French and Indian War.

Johnston, Mary. *Croatan.* **Little, 1923.**
A story of the tragic Roanoke colony of 1587.

Johnston, Mary. *Prisoners of hope.* **Houghton, 1898.**
About the English convicts who were sent to Virginia around 1650.

Johnston, Mary. *To have and to hold.* **Houghton, 1900.**
An old and favorite romance about the importation of wives into
Virginia in 1619.

Longstreet, Stephen. *War in the golden weather.* **Doubleday, 1965.**
Colorful novel about a young and hopeful painter in colonial America
who follows Major Washington in the campaigns against the
French and Indians.

129

Marsh, George. *Ask no quarter.* **Morrow, 1945.**
Plenty of action with Indians, pirates and so on, in colonial Rhode Island.

Mason, Van Wyck. *The Sea 'venture.* **Doubleday, 1961.**
Engrossing story of the ship which sailed for Jamestown in 1609 and was wrecked in Bermuda by a storm.

Mason, Van Wyck. *Young titan.* **Doubleday, 1959.**
A novel of King William's War and the New England settlers' attempt to capture the French stronghold of Louisbourg.

Mayrant, Drayton. *Land beyond the tempest.* **Coward, 1959.**
Story about a Cornish girl who sails on her father's ship, *Sea Venture,* for Jamestown. It is wrecked on Bermuda.

Miers, Earl S. *Valley in arms.* **Westminster, 1943.**
A story of two young people who built a house in the Connecticut River valley in early colonial times when the area was subject to frequent Indian raids.

Pangborn, Edgar. *Wilderness of spring.* **Rinehart, 1958.**
Story about two orphaned brothers in early 18th century New England, one of whom goes to sea and the other becomes a physician.

Phillips, Alexandra. *Forever possess.* **Dutton, 1946.**
About the great Hudson River estates in the 1690's and Leisler's rebellion. Good picture of the period and setting.

Raddall, Thomas. *The governor's lady.* **Doubleday, 1959.**
A novel about John Wentworth, the last royal governor of New Hampshire, and his wife.

Rees, Gilbert. *I seek a city.* **Dutton, 1950.**
A first person novel about the life of Roger Williams, founder of Rhode Island.

Ritchie, Cicero. *Willing maid.* **Abelard, 1958.**
Tale of adventure in 18th century Nova Scotia, culminating in the
fall of Louisbourg.

Roberts, Kenneth. *Northwest passage.* **Doubleday, 1937.**
The period is that of the French and Indian War and the descriptive
action is masterly. Major Robert Rogers, of the famous Rangers, is
one of the two chief characters.

Schachner, Nathan. *King's passenger.* **Lippincott, 1942.**
A young Englishman, deported to colonial Virginia, has Nathaniel
Bacon as a fellow-passenger and later joins him in rebellion against
the governor.

Schofield, William. *Ashes in the wilderness.* **Macrae Smith, 1942.**
Graphic portrayal of King Phillip's War in Rhode Island and
Massachusetts.

Scruggs, Philip. *Man cannot tell.* **Bobbs, 1942.**
A story of colonial Virginia and Bacon's Rebellion.

Seton, Anya. *The Winthrop woman.* **Houghton, 1958.**
Based on the life of Elizabeth Winthrop, niece of the governor of
the Massachusetts Bay Colony. Good portrayal of early colonial life.

Settle, Mary Lee. *O Beulah land.* **Viking, 1956.**
Story of a Virginia gentleman who, in the 1770's, leads the first
settlers over the mountains into the western wilderness of what would
some day be West Virginia.

Speare, Elizabeth. *The prospering.* **Houghton, 1967.**
Well-written story set in 18th century Stockbridge, Massachusetts.
Good characterizations and background.

Stone, Grace. *Cold journey.* **Morrow, 1934.**
Vivid classic of the Deerfield Massacre in 1704 and of the captives'
terrible journey to Quebec.

Stover, Herbert. *Song of the Susquehanna.* **Dodd, 1949.**
The adventures and romance of a Pennsylvania German during the French and Indian War. Especially good in local color.

Sublette, Clifford. *Bright face of danger.* **Little, 1926.**
A story of Bacon's Rebellion in colonial Virginia.

Swanson, Neil. *First rebel.* **Farrar, 1937.**
Good historical novel about Col. James Smith and the Scotch-Irish settlers in 18th century Pennsylvania who were strongly anti-British. Vivid account of Braddock's defeat and other events of that period.

Swanson, Neil. *Judas tree.* **Putnam, 1933.**
Romance and action in the defense of Fort Pitt during the Conspiracy of Pontiac.

Tracy, Don. *Carolina corsair.* **Dial, 1955.**
Melodrama and action in this story about Edward Teach, the pirate known as Blackbeard in the 1770's.

Van de Water, Frederic. *Reluctant rebel.* **Duell, 1948.**
Good novel of the Green Mountain Boys and the rivalry between New York and New Hampshire over Vermont just before the Revolution.

Walz, Jay and Audrey. *Bizarre sisters.* **Duell, 1950.**
Well-written fictionalized account of an actual scandal and family feud that involved the Randolphs of Virginia in the late 18th century.

Whitson, Denton. *Governor's daughter.* **Bobbs, 1952.**
Adventure and romance during the French and Indian War, with the daughter of Governor Delancey of New York as the heroine.

Widdemer, Margaret. *Lady of the Mohawks.* **Doubleday, 1951.**
Romantic story of the lives of Molly Brant and her husband, the English proprieter, Sir William Johnson. Setting is upper New York State during the French and Indian War.

Winwar, Frances. *Gallows Hill.* **Holt, 1937.**
The Salem witchcraft hysteria.

Wyckoff, Nicholas E. *The Braintree mission.* **Macmillan, 1957.**
The story is set in Boston in 1770, and revolves around a supposed effort by the British government to stop unrest by offering earldoms to six colonial leaders. In this case, the story concentrates on John and Abigail Adams.

Zara, Louis. *Blessed is the land.* **Crown, 1954.**
Tells the story of the first Jewish migrants to America, a group who settled in New Amsterdam in 1654.

JUVENILE

Alderman, Clifford. *Vengeance of Abel Wright.* **Doubleday, 1964.**
Story of two boys captured by Indians in King Philip's War in 1675 and of their escape.

Aldis, Dorothy. *Ride the wild waves.* **Putnam, 1957.**
Based on fact, a story of two English children who come to colonial Massachusetts.

Allen, Merritt P. *Flicker's feather.* **Longmans, 1952.**
A story of the French and Indian War around Lake Champlain, with several good characterizations.

Best, Allena. *Seven beaver skins.* **Winston, 1948.**
About a Dutch boy, skilled in sorting beaver pelts, who comes to New Netherlands and lives through its brief history.

Best, Herbert. *Long portage.* **Viking, 1948.**
Exciting tale about a New York boy who runs away to join Rogers' Rangers in the French and Indian War.

Best, Herbert. *Ranger's ransom.* Aladdin, 1953.
The French and Indian War, and especially the fighting for Fort Ticonderoga.

Bothwell, Jean. *Lady of Roanoke.* Holt, 1965.
A fictional explanation of the fate of Virginia Dare and the lost colony of Roanoke.

Bowers, Gwendolyn. *Journey for Jemima.* Walck, 1960.
Exciting story of a New England girl captured by Indians, and rescued by a French trapper. She eventually gets home, aided by a boy she had known.

Butters, Dorothy G. *Girl in buckskin.* Macrae Smith, 1956.
Set in New England in early colonial days, it is a story about how a girl survived the dangers of a wilderness journey.

Cooke, Donald. *Little wolf slayer.* Winston, 1952.
Story of a young boy who takes part in the Quaker settlement of Philadelphia.

Denker, Nan. *Bound girl.* Farrar, 1957.
Story for girls about a French orphan girl who lives as a bound servant with a Puritan family near Boston.

Desmond, Alice. *George Washington's mother.* Dodd, 1961.
Fictionalized biography of Mary Ball.

Dobler, Lavinia. *Glass house at Jamestown.* Dodd, 1957.
About a teen-age boy in early Jamestown who learns the glass-blower's craft there.

Duncan, John M. *Down the mast road.* McGraw, 1956.
Story about a boy in colonial New Hampshire who has the task of cutting down a tall pine for a mast and getting it out of the forest.

Emery, Anne. *A spy in old Detroit.* **Rand McNally, 1963.**
A boy acts as a British spy during Pontiac's War of 1763.

Faulkner, Nancy. *Tomahawk shadow.* **Doubleday, 1959.**
Good story of a boy's adventures in Providence in the days of Roger Williams and of King Phillip's War.

Finney, Gertrude. *Is this my love.* **Longmans, 1956.**
A story for girls about the shipload of English girls who were sent to Jamestown in 1619 as wives for the settlers.

Finney, Gertrude. *Muskets along the Chickahominy.* **Longmans, 1953.**
A novel about Bacon's Rebellion in colonial Virginia. Strong historical background.

Latham, Jean. *This dear-bought land.* **Harper, 1956.**
Excellent story about a boy's part in the settlement of Jamestown and his friendship with Captain John Smith.

Lobdell, Helen. *Captain Bacon's rebellion.* **Macrae Smith, 1959.**
Romance and adventure as part of Bacon's Rebellion in colonial Virginia.

Lobdell, Helen. *Fort in the forest.* **Houghton, 1963.**
Exciting story of two French boys who take part in a winter expedition aganist the Indians in the days of New France and the conflict with England.

Mason, Miriam. *Three ships came sailing in.* **Bobbs, 1950.**
A story of the settlement of Jamestown.

Meigs, Cornelia. *Two arrows.* **Macmillan, 1949.**
About two English boys who come to Maryland in 1745.

Miers, Earl S. *Pirate chase.* **Holt, 1965.**
Adventure story of colonial times about a youth who, sailing from Williamsburg to England, is captured by pirates. Later he aids in their seizure.

Patton, Willoughby. *Sea Venture.* **Longmans, 1959.**
Story of an English boy's voyage to Jamestown in 1609 and of the shipwreck on Bermuda.

Petry, Ann. *Tituba of Salem village.* **Crowell, 1964.**
Good story about a Negro slave caught up in the Salem witchcraft hysteria. Based on fact.

Robinson, Gertrude. *The mooring tree.* **Oxford U. P., 1957.**
A boy's adventures in the Jamestown colony.

Robinson, Gertrude. *Sign of the Golden Fish.* **Winston, 1949.**
A good account of the 17th century Cornish fishermen who came to Maine and founded the fishing industry there.

Speare, Elizabeth. *Witch of Blackbird Pond.* **Houghton, 1958.**
Story of a 17th century New England girl who rebels against the harsh Puritan beliefs.

Steele, William. *Trail through danger.* **Harcourt, 1965.**
Adventure story of a colonial hunting party which is ambushed by Indians.

Strachan, Winona. *Christopher Jarrett of New Plymouth.* **Dutton, 1957.**
A boy from London lives in the Pilgrim colony in New England. Good junior high school background story.

Welch, Ronald. *Mohawk Valley.* **Criterion, 1958.**
Fast-moving story of a young Englishman in the French and Indian War.

THE REVOLUTIONARY PERIOD

Alderman, Clifford. *Arch of stars.* **Appleton, 1950.**
A lively story of the Revolutionary War in Vermont, including of course, Ethan Allen.

Allis, Marguerite. *Now we are free.* **Putnam, 1952.**
A story of several Connecticut Revolutionary War veterans who, after the war, must decide whether to return home to farm their land, or to go west.

Bacheller, Irving. *In the days of Poor Richard.* **Bobbs, 1922.**
A novel of the Revolutionary period, and especially a good portrait of Franklin.

Barker, Shirley. *The fire and the hammer.* **Crown, 1953.**
Revolutionary War story, set in Pennsylvania and New Jersey, about a family of Tory sympathizers who made private war on the patriots.

Barker, Shirley. *Last gentleman.* **Random, 1960.**
Romance set in New England just before the outbreak of the Revolution, when loyalties were being strained.

Barry, Jane. *The Carolinians.* **Doubleday, 1959.**
Revolutionary War in the South; Battles of Cowpens and King's Mountain.

Barry, Jane. *Long march.* **Appleton, 1955.**
Good story of the Revolution in the South, particularly of General Morgan and the Battle of Cowpens.

Bernard, Paul. *Genesee Castle.* **Dorrance, 1970.**
A story of the Revolutionary War, dealing with Sullivan's raid against the Iroquois in central New York.

137

Beverley-Giddings, Arthur. *Rival shores.* **Morrow, 1956.**
Romance set on the Eastern Shore of Maryland just before the Revolution, and dealing with escaping Loyalist refugees.

Boyce, Burke. *Man from Mt. Vernon.* **Harper, 1961.**
Fictionalized picture of Washington's military career during the
Revolution. Good characterization.

Boyce, Burke. *Perilous night.* **Viking, 1942.**
A novel of the American Revolution, dealing with a family in the
Hudson River area where Whigs and Tories were closely intermixed.

Boyd, James. *Drums.* **Scribner, 1925.**
A stirring story of the Revolution in the South. John Paul Jones and
Daniel Morgan are important figures.

Brick, John. *King's rangers.* **Doubleday, 1954.**
Tells of the American Revolution in New York State from the Tory
point-of-view.

Brick, John. *The raid.* **Farrar, 1951.**
American Revolutionary story about a family in the Mohawk Valley
subjected to Indian and Tory attacks.

Brick, John. *The rifleman.* **Doubleday, 1953.**
The hero is Timothy Murphy, an actual figure in the Revolution in
upper New York. He was a rough, unlettered but fascinating
woodsman involved in plenty of action.

Brick, John. *Strong men.* **Doubleday, 1959.**
Story of the Revolutionary War, especially Valley Forge and
Monmouth.

Bristow, Gwen. *Celia Garth.* **Crowell, 1959.**
Romance and intrigue involve a young woman in the Revolutionary
War in South Carolina. Much action.

Chambers, Robert W. *Little red foot.* **Doran, 1921.**
Story of Indian warfare in New York during the Revolution.

Chapman, Maristan. *Rogue's march.* **Lippincott, 1949.**
Story of the Revolution in the South, especially of the Battle of
King's Mountain.

Churchill, Winston. *The crossing.* **Macmillan, 1904.**
The Kentucky frontier during the Revolution, and Clark's conquest
of the Northwest Territory.

Churchill, Winston. *Richard Carvel.* **Macmillan, 1899.**
One of the classic novels of the American Revolution.

Davis, Burke. *The ragged ones.* **Rinehart, 1951.**
Story about the activities of American soldiers under Greene and
Morgan fighting in the southern campaigns of the Revolution.

Davis, William S. *Gilman of Redford.* **Macmillan, 1927.**
Boston at the opening of the Revolution as seen by a Harvard student. Excellent background and atmosphere.

Desmond, Alice. *Alexander Hamilton's wife.* **Dodd, 1952.**
Biographical novel of Betsy Schuyler; of interest to women and
older girls.

Edmonds, Walter D. *Drums along the Mohawk.* **Little, 1936.**
Famous and exciting story of the Revolutionary War and Indian
fighting in New York State.

Ehle, John. *The land breakers.* **Harper, 1963.**
Story of pioneers in the California-Tennessee mountains around
1780. Good action and background.

139

Ellsberg, Edward. *Captain Paul.* **Dodd, 1941.**
Biographical novel about John Paul Jones, strongly realistic in its
scenes of naval action.

Fast, Howard. *April morning.* **Crown, 1961.**
Story about a boy on the day of Lexington and Concord. Good picture of the impact of the British raid. For teen-agers and adults.

Fast, Howard. *Citizen Tom Paine.* **Duell, 1943.**
A fictionalized biography of a revolutionary, told with sincerity and
vividness.

Fast, Howard. *Conceived in liberty.* **Simon & Schuster, 1939.**
Valley Forge in the Revolution; realistic picture with social implica-
tions in contrasting the gentlemen officers from the common soldiers.

Fast, Howard. *The proud and the free.* **Little, 1950.**
A novel about the mutiny of a regiment of Pennsylvania troops on
January 1, 1781, as the author interprets their grievances.

Fast, Howard. *The unvanquished.* **Duell, 1942.**
A novel about Washington in the darkest days of the Revolution,
showing his growth from a Virginia farmer to a decisive leader.

Feuchtwanger, Lion. *Proud destiny.* **Viking, 1947.**
A long and historically sound novel dealing with Franklin's years in
Paris seeking French aid for the colonists.

Fletcher, Inglis. *Toil of the brave.* **Bobbs, 1946.**
Story of the Revolution in North Carolina in 1779, and the Battle
of King's Mountain.

Flood, Charles. *Monmouth.* **Houghton, 1961.**
A good story of the Revolution, starting with Valley Forge and ending at Monmouth. Historical realism and believable characters.

Ford, Paul Leicester. *Janice Meredith*. Dodd, 1899.
One of the classic romantic novels of the American Revolution.

Frye, Pearl. *Gallant captain*. Little, 1956.
Well-written novel of the career of John Paul Jones.

Gerson, Noel. *I'll storm hell*. Doubleday, 1967.
Biographical novel on the career of Revolutionary General Anthony
Wayne.

Gerson, Noel. *The swamp fox*. Doubleday, 1967.
Good fictional biography of General Francis Marion, the Revolutionary hero in the Carolinas.

Gessner, Robert. *Treason*. Scribner, 1944.
Well-written novel of Benedict Arnold, seen through the eyes of one
of his aides.

Graves, Robert. *Proceed, Sergeant Lamb*. Random, 1941.
The sergeant becomes a prisoner of war, escapes to join Cornwallis
and is involved in the surrender at Yorktown.

Graves, Robert. *Sergeant Lamb's America*. Random, 1940.
An Irish soldier in the British army comes to America as part of the
forces attempting to subdue the colonists. He describes his experiences and impressions.

Haislip, Harvey. *Prize master*. Doubleday, 1959.
Story of an American midshipman in the Revolution who is put in
charge of a ship captured by privateers. Full of action, especially
suitable for teen-agers.

Haislip, Harvey. *Sailor named Jones*. Doubleday, 1957.
Centering around the naval career of John Paul Jones, this novel
has unusually authentic maritime settings.

Haislip, Harvey. *Sea road to Yorktown*. Doubleday, 1960.
Sequel to *The Prize Master,* dealing with the naval blockade of Cornwallis at Yorktown.

Harris, Cyril. *Richard Pryne*. Scribner, 1941.
Good novel of a civilian who acts as a spy for General Washington.

Heckert, Eleanor. *The golden rock*. Doubleday, 1970.
A novel of the American Revolution about the island of St. Eustatius in the Caribbean, a pirate stronghold and a port through which the colonial army got supplies through the British blockade.

Henri, Florette. *Kings Mountain*. Doubleday, 1950.
Revolutionary War novel centering in the Battle of King's Mountain in 1780.

Hopkins, J. G. E. *Patriot's progress*. Scribner, 1961.
Problems of divided loyalties at the outbreak of the American Revolution, among family and friends.

Horan, James. *King's rebel*. Crown, 1953.
Indian fighting and the Cherry Valley massacre in New York State during the Revolution.

Horne, Howard. *Concord bridge*. Bobbs, 1952.
Story of the opening scenes of the Revolution.

Hough, Frank. *The neutral ground*. Lippincott, 1941.
Highly interesting novel of the American Revolution, set in Westchester County, New York, where irregular troops of both sides ranged the countryside.

Hough, Frank. *Renown*. Carrick, 1938.
Long and historically sound novel about Benedict Arnold.

Jennings, John. *Sea eagles.* **Doubleday, 1950.**
Story of the American Revolution, particularly good in its seafaring atmosphere.

Jordan, Mildred. *Echo of the flute.* **Doubleday, 1958.**
Story of a Philadelphia family during the Revolution and in the yellow fever epidemic of 1793.

Karig, Walter and Bird, Horace. *Don't tread on me.* **Rinehart, 1954.**
An historical novel about John Paul Jones, with plenty of action and authentic seafaring background.

Lancaster, Bruce. *Big knives.* **Little, 1964.**
Story of George Rogers Clark's conquest of the Northwest Territory in 1778, as seen by a young merchant on the expedition.

Lancaster, Bruce. *Blind journey.* **Little, 1953.**
A story of the Revolutionary War, particularly good for historical background.

Lancaster, Bruce. *Guns of Burgoyne.* **Stokes, 1939.**
Unusually good story of the Saratoga campaign with the protagonist being a young Hessian officer.

Lancaster, Bruce. *Phantom fortress.* **Little, 1950.**
A novel of the American Revolution in the South in 1780, especially of General Marion's fast-moving forces. Action and romance, well-told.

Lancaster, Bruce. *Secret road.* **Little, 1952.**
Interesting and authentic novel about Revolutionary espionage on Long Island in 1780.

Lancaster, Bruce. *Trumpet to arms.* **Little, 1944.**
Vigorous story of the Revolution, showing how rural militia developed into fighting soldiers. Battles of Trenton and Princeton.

143

Leland, John A. *Othneil Jones.* **Lippincott, 1956.**
Action-filled story of a young man, part white and part Cherokee, who fights with Marion's raiders in 1781 in Tennessee.

Linington, Elizabeth. *Long watch.* **Viking, 1956.**
Set in New York City during the Revolution, it deals particularly with public opinion as seen by a young newspaperman.

Longstreet, Stephen. *A few painted feathers.* **Doubleday, 1963.**
Good story of the Revolutionary War with the action set in South Carolina. Background and plot are interesting and realistic. Chief character is the Surgeon-General.

Mason, Van Wyck. *Eagle in the sky.* **Lippincott, 1948.**
Story of the American Revolution in 1780, combining vivid sea adventure and medical practice.

Mason, Van Wyck. *Rivers of glory.* **Lippincott, 1942.**
A vivid novel of the American Revolution, set partly in Jamaica and partly at the siege of Savannah.

Mason, Van Wyck. *Stars on the sea.* **Lippincott, 1940.**
Exciting and colorful story of colonial privateering activity during the first two years of the Revolution.

Mason, Van Wyck. *Three harbours.* **Lippincott, 1938.**
Long and colorful novel of the early days of the American Revolution, with a great deal of action. The harbours are Boston, Norfolk and Bermuda.

Mercer, Charles. *Enough good men.* **Putnam, 1959.**
A long story of romance and realistic background in Philadelphia during the Revolution, showing much of the impact of war on ordinary people.

Mitchell, S. Weir. *Hugh Wynne, Free Quaker.* **Century, 1897.**
An old but long-popular novel of Philadelphia life during the Revolution.

Morrow, Honore. *Let the King beware!* Morrow, 1936.
Unusual novel depicting the revolt of the American colonies from the point-of-view of George III, Lord North and the Tory leaders.

Nutt, Frances. *Three fields to cross.* Stephen-Paul, 1947.
A novel of a family on Staten Island, New York, during the American Revolution.

Page, Elizabeth. *Tree of liberty.* Holt, 1939.
Good historical fiction involving the Revolutionary and Constitutional period, and stressing the conflict between the ideas of Hamilton and Jefferson.

Rayner, William. *World turned upside down.* Morrow, 1970.
Story of the American Revolution. A British officer seeking to escape from rebel captors in Virginia stains his skin to pass as a slave, and finds that freedom means different things to different people.

Roberts, Kenneth. *Arundel.* Doubleday, 1930.
Vivid story of Arnold's attempt to capture Quebec in the early days of the Revolution.

Roberts, Kenneth. *Oliver Wiswell.* Doubleday, 1940.
This long novel of the American Revolution is quite different from most, in that the hero is a Loyalist and the reader sees the whole war as Loyalists saw it.

Roberts, Kenneth. *Rabble in arms.* Doubleday, 1933.
Long but vivid and exciting novel about the Saratoga campaign, with a favorable picture of Arnold.

Sabatini, Rafael. *The Carolinian.* Houghton, 1925.
Story of the American Revolution in South Carolina.

Schoonover, Lawrence. *The revolutionary.* Little, 1958.
Based on the career of John Paul Jones, and filled with action.

145

Schumann, Mary. *Strife before dawn.* **Dial, 1939.**
Good historical detail as well as action in this account of American conquest of the Old Northwest, above the Ohio.

Seifert, Shirley. *Waters of the wilderness.* **Lippincott, 1941.**
Romance and vivid action in this novel about George Rogers Clark who conquered the land north of the Ohio during the Revolution.

Simons, Katherine. *Red doe.* **Appleton, 1953.**
Story of General Francis Marion, the Revolution's "swamp fox."

Sinclair, Harold. *Westward the tide.* **Doubleday, 1940.**
A novel about George Rogers Clark and his expedition to capture Vincennes during the American Revolution.

Slaughter, Frank G. *Flight from Natchez.* **Doubleday, 1955.**
Story set in Florida in the last years of the American Revolution.

Spicer, Bart. *Brother to the enemy.* **Dodd, 1958.**
Based on fact, the story of a young American soldier in the Revolution who undertakes the mission of trying to recapture Benedict Arnold from the British in New York.

Stanley, Edward. *Thomas Forty.* **Duell, 1947.**
Story of a bound boy in New York's Westchester County during the Revolution, who joins up with the local partisan fighters against the Tories.

Sterne, Emma. *Drums of Monmouth.* **Dodd, 1935.**
Revolutionary War story set in New Jersey and New York, stressing the activities of the poet, Philip Freneau.

Stover, Herbert. *Men in buckskin.* **Dodd, 1950.**
Story set during the Revolution and dealing with the Indian and British raids on settlers in the Susquehanna Valley of Pennsylvania.

Stover, Herbert. *Powder mission.* Dodd, 1951.
Exciting story of an American expedition in the Revolution going
down the rivers to New Orleans for ammunition for the patriot army.

Swanson, Neil. *The first rebel.* Farrar, 1937.
Anti-British activities of Scotch-Irish settlers in Pennsylvania just
before the Revolution.

Taylor, David. *Farewell to Valley Forge.* Lippincott, 1955.
Good historical fiction about two young patriots acting as Washington's spies in 1778.

Taylor, David. *Lights across the Delaware.* Lippincott, 1954.
Good exciting story about the Americans' capture of Trenton in 1776.

Taylor, David. *Storm the last rampart.* Lippincott, 1960.
About a patriot spy operating among the British in Westchester
County, New York, during the last years of the Revolution.

Taylor, David. *Sycamore men.* Lippincott, 1958.
American Revolution, with Francis Marion and his men in the
southern campaigns.

Turnbull, Agnes. *Day must dawn.* Macmillan, 1942.
Enjoyable novel about a family in a small town in Pennsylvania
during the Revolution.

Ven de Water, Frederick. *Day of battle.* Washburn, 1958.
The Revolution in Vermont — Ticonderoga to Bennington.

Van Every, Dale. *Bridal journey.* Messner, 1950.
Well-written story of a girl's adventures with Indians, Tories and
other people during the Revolution in frontier Ohio.

Van Every, Dale. *Captive witch.* Messner, 1951.
George Rogers Clark, the pioneer West, and vivid battle scenes
during the Revolution.

Vaughan, Carter. *Scoundrels' brigade.* **Doubleday, 1962.**

Romantic and fast-moving adventure story about a unit formed by General Washington to track down British counterfeiters of Continental currency.

Vining, Elizabeth. *Virginia exiles.* **Lippincott, 1955.**

About the Philadelphia Quakers at the time of the Revolution.

JUVENILE

Allen, Merritt. *Battle lanterns.* **Longmans, 1949.**

Exciting events during the Revolution, involving a boy's adventures as a captive in the West Indies and as a member of General Marion's forces in the South.

Bell, Kensil. *Secret mission for Valley Forge.* **Dodd, 1955.**

Story of a boy who guided a foraging expedition for General Anthony Wayne to get supplies for Washington.

Best, A. C. *Wavering flame.* **Scribner, 1953.**

Set in Litchfield, Connecticut, at the time of the Revolution, it is a good story about a printer's apprentice.

Beyer, Audrey. *Katherine Leslie.* **Knopf, 1963.**

Young English girl escapes from London prison to America, becomes involved in the outbreak of the Revolution and the burning of Falmouth, Maine, in 1775. Exciting story for girls.

Brick, John. *Eagle of Niagara.* **Doubleday, 1955.**

Story of the Revolution. A patriot soldier is captured by the Indian, Joseph Brant. Good picture of conflicting points-of-view.

Butters, Dorothy. *The bells of freedom.* **Macrae Smith, 1963.**

Lively story of a bound boy in Revolutionary Boston who is apprenticed to a counterfeiter.

Clagett, John. *Gunpowder for Boonesborough.* **Bobbs, 1965.**

Story of Indian fighters in 1776 on a journey down the Mississippi to New Orleans for gunpowder. Action and thrills.

Clarke, Mary. *Petticoat rebel.* **Viking, 1964.**
During the Revolution in Gloucester, Massachusetts, a young girl is asked to teach school, and insists on having a Negro girl among her pupils.

Cluff, Tom. *Minutemen of the sea.* **Follett, 1955.**
How a group of Maine patriots seized a British cutter in the early months of the Revolution.

Coolidge, Olivia. *Cromwell's head.* **Houghton, 1955.**
A story set in Revolutionary Boston, in which a young surgeon's apprentice becomes involved in romance and conflicting loyalties.

Dean, Leon. *Royalton raid.* **Rinehart, 1949.**
About a Vermont boy captured by Indians and British during the Revolution, and how he escaped.

Decker, Malcolm. *Rebel and the turncoat.* **McGraw, 1949.**
A story good for teen-agers or adults about a young man who for a time could not decide whether to side with the tories or the rebels during the Revolution. A girl from each party helped him make up his mind.

Dick, Trella. *Flag in hiding.* **Abelard, 1959.**
An American Revolution story of a family living among Tories but secretly aiding the patriot cause.

Dilliard, Maud. *Ahoy, Peggy Stewart!* **Dutton, 1956.**
A lively story of the resistance of Maryland people to the British tax on tea just before the Revolution.

Duncan, John. *Twelve days 'til Trenton.* **McGraw, 1957.**
Story of two boys in the Continental Army just before and during the Battle of Trenton.

Emery, Anne. *Spy in old Philadelphia.* **Rand McNally, 1958.**
Adventures of a patriot boy in the early years of the Revolution.

149

Emery, Anne. *Spy in old West Point*. Rand McNally, 1965.
Story of a boy who becomes involved in the capture of Andre.

Faulkner, Nancy. *Undecided heart*. Doubleday, 1956.
Girl's story of divided family loyalties in Virginia during the American Revolution.

Forbes, Esther. *Johnny Tremaine*. Houghton, 1943.
Outstanding story of a boy involved in the beginnings of the Revolution around Boston.

Forman, James. *The Cow Neck rebels*. Farrar, 1970.
Good Revolutionary War novel, in which the Battle of Long Island is the central event, and affects the lives of the principal characters.

Groh, Lynn. *The Culper spy ring*. Westminster, 1970.
Interesting story based on fact, of the espionage activities of a group of American patriots in Long Island and Connecticut during the Revolution.

Havighurst, Walter. *Proud prisoner*. Holt, 1964.
Story about Henry Hamilton, British governor of Detroit during the Revolution, who paid Indians to bring him American scalps.

Hungerford, Edward. *Forge for heroes*. Wilcox, 1952.
Revolutionary War at Valley Forge.

James, Norma. *Dawn at Lexington*. Longmans, 1957.
A Boston bookseller's apprentice is involved in the exciting events at the outbreak of the Revolution.

Kent, Louise. *He went with John Paul Jones*. Houghton, 1957.
Adventures of a teen-age Virginia boy who not only served under Jones, but also sailed around the world with Capt. Cook.

Lawrence, Isabelle. *Spy in Williamsburg*. Rand McNally, 1955.
Story of a young boy who helps save the town from the British during the Revolution.

Lawson, Robert. *Mr. Revere and I.* Little, 1953.
Clever and amusing story of Revere and the Revolution as purportedly seen and told by his horse.

Levy, Mimi. *Whaleboat warriors.* Viking, 1963.
How a group of boys, white and Negro, carry a message across Long Island Sound through British lines.

Meadowcroft, Enid. *Silver for General Washington.* Crowell, 1957.
Two young patriot refugees from Philadelphia steal back into the city to recover the family silver and give the proceeds of its sale to Washington at Valley Forge.

Nelson, May. *Redbirds are flying.* Criterion, 1963.
Revolutionary War. A boy aids General Nathanael Greene with valuable information.

Patterson, Emma. *Midnight patriot.* Longmans, 1949.
Good story of the Revolution in the Hudson River valley.

Savage, Josephine. *Gunpowder girl.* Day, 1958.
Teen-age Boston girl in 1775 becomes involved in a plot to secretly manufacture gunpowder for the rebels.

Savery, Constance. *The Reb and the redcoats.* Longmans, 1961.
Story of an English family whose father is in America fighting the rebels in the Revolution. Billeted with them is a 15-year old Virginian, a prisoner of war, anxious to escape. Interesting and fresh approach to the Revolutionary period.

Sentman, George. *Drummer of Vincennes.* Winston, 1952.
Adventure story about George Rogers Clark's conquest of the Northwest Territory during the Revolution.

Singmaster, Elsie. *Rifles for Washington.* Houghton, 1938.
Excellent story of a boy and his uncle who serve together in Washington's army.

Thane, Elswyth. *Dawn's early light.* **Duell, 1943.**
Pleasant romantic story of Williamsburg, Virginia, during the period of the Revolution.

Voight, Virginia. *Girl from Johnnycake Hill.* **Prentice, 1961.**
Good story for girls about a girl and her mother in Connecticut in 1780, involved in the settlement of land disputes with the Indians.

Webb, Christopher. *Matt Tyler's chronicle.* **Funk, 1958.**
Adventures of an apprentice boy fighting for the patriot army in the Revolution.

Wibberley, Leonard. *John Treegate's musket.* **Farrar, 1959.**
Good story about a young apprentice involved in the divided loyalties in Boston shortly before the Revolution.

Wibberley, Leonard. *Peter Treegate's war.* **Ariel, 1960.**
Second in a trilogy about the Treegate family in the Revolution. Peter escapes from a British prison to join the American army at the Battle of Trenton.

Wibberley, Leonard. *Sea captain from Salem.* **Farrar, 1961.**
Good story of privateering in British waters during the American Revolution.

Wibberley, Leonard. *Treegate's raiders.* **Ariel, 1962.**
Another adventure of Peter Treegate, who goes to South Carolina and eventually sees Cornwallis's surrender at Yorktown.

Wilson, Charles. *Sentry in the night.* **Washburn, 1953.**
Story of a young Hessian soldier in the American Revolution.

Wilson, Charles. *The winds blow free.* **Washburn, 1950.**
A lively adventure story of a boy on an American privateer during the Revolution.

1789-1860

Adams, Samuel H. *Banner by the wayside.* **Random, 1947.**
Pleasant tale of two young men in a theatrical touring group along
the Erie Canal in its heyday.

Adams, Samuel H. *Gorgeous hussy.* **Houghton, 1934.**
Story about Peggy O'Neale and the politics of Andrew Jackson's
cabinet.

Allis, Marguerite. *Brave pursuit.* **Putnam, 1954.**
Good picture of pioneer life in Ohio in the early 1800's, and a story
of a girl's efforts to get a good education.

Allis, Marguerite. *Free soil.* **Putnam, 1957.**
The Kansas frontier in the 1850's when settlers were bitterly divided
over slavery.

Allis, Marguerite. *Rising storm.* **Putnam, 1955.**
The underground railroad and abolition movement in Ohio.

Allis, Marguerite. *Splendor stays.* **Putnam, 1942.**
The story of the seven daughters of Captain Hart of Saybrook, Connecticut, who, in the early 1800's, made some notable marriages and
traveled widely.

Banks, Polan. *Black ivory.* **Harper, 1926.**
About Jean Lafitte, pirate and slave trader.

Best, Herbert. *Young'un.* **Macmillan, 1944.**
A pleasant story of how a family of children on Lake Champlain just
after the Revolution fended for themselves when deprived of their
parents. Enjoyable setting.

Breslin, Howard. *Shad run.* **Crowell, 1955.**
A story of the Hudson River Valley in 1788, stressing the struggle
over the ratification of the new Constitution and the importance of
the fishing industry.

Breslin, Howard. *Tamarack tree.* **McGraw, 1947.**
Small town in New England during the exciting political campaign of 1840.

Case, Josephine. *Written in sand.* **Houghton, 1945.**
Story of the American war against the Barbary pirates of Tripoli.

Chapman, Maristan. *Tennessee hazard.* **Lippincott, 1952.**
Early pioneer days in the old Southwest, when Spanish influence was still felt.

Cicchetti, Janet. *O Genesee.* **Lippincott, 1957.**
Story of pioneering in western New York before and during the War of 1812.

Crabb, Alfred. *Home to Kentucky.* **Bobbs, 1953.**
A biography of Henry Clay in fiction form.

David, Evan. *As runs the glass.* **Harper, 1943.**
An exciting story of the seafaring adventures of a Maine family in the last years of the 18th century.

Davidson, Louis and Doherty, Edward. *Captain Marooner.* **Crowell, 1952.**
Story of a mutiny on a Nantucket whaler in 1822, based on fact.

Davis, Dorothy S. *Men of no property.* **Scribner, 1955.**
Good account of the arrival of a group of Irish immigrants to New York in 1848 and of their experiences during the next two decades. Realistic.

Davis, Harold. *Beulah land.* **Morrow, 1949.**
A fascinating account of the long and dangerous journey of two young people in the early 1800's as they wandered through the mid-west frontier in search of a home for themselves.

Davis, Julia. *Cloud on the land.* **Rinehart, 1951.**
Historical romance of the early 19th century in which a young woman who is opposed to slavery marries a Virginia slave-holder and goes to be mistress of his plantation.

Davis, Paxton. *The seasons of heroes.* **Morrow, 1967.**
Really three stories in one, as three generations of a Virginia family recall major crises in the past. Military life in the 19th century is prominent; old-fashioned virtues of honor, courage and justice are stressed.

Desmond, Alice. *Bewitching Betsy Bonaparte.* **Dodd, 1958.**
About the American girl who married Napoleon's brother, Jerome.

Edwards, Samuel. *Barbary general.* **Prentice, 1968.**
Biographical novel about General William Eaton, an American soldier who did much to settle our troubles with the pirates of North Africa in the early 1800's.

Ehrlich, Leonard. *God's angry man.* **Simon & Schuster, 1932.**
Vivid novel about the abolitionist, John Brown.

Ellis, William. *Bounty lands.* **World, 1952.**
Excellent fictional treatment of the settlement of the Ohio territory just after the Revolution.

Fletcher, Inglis. *Queen's gift.* **Bobbs, 1952.**
A story of a South Carolina plantation in the years just after the Revolution.

Forester, C. S. *Captain from Connecticut.* **Little, 1941.**
Fine sea story of the War of 1812.

Fuller, Edmund. *Star pointed north.* **Harper, 1946.**
Well-written fictionalized biography of Frederick Douglass, the slave who became a famous northern Abolitionist leader.

Furnas, J. C. *Devil's rainbow.* **Harper, 1962.**
Fictionalized story of Joseph Smith, the founder of Mormonism. Sensational but controversial in its point-of-view.

Gerson, Noel. *Cumberland Rifles.* **Doubleday, 1952.**
Tennessee just after the Revolution.

Gerson, Noel. *The Golden Eagle.* **Doubleday, 1953.**
Good historical novel about the Mexican War.

Harris, Cyril. *Street of knives.* **Little, 1950.**
Aaron Burr's mysterious and sinister enterprise in the Mississippi country in 1806 is the subject.

Hepburn, Andrew. *Letter of marque.* **Little, 1959.**
Story of a group of Yankee seamen who escape from impressment on a British ship and man their own privateer in the War of 1812. Good sailing ship background.

Hodge, Jane Aiken. *Here comes a candle.* **Doubleday, 1967.**
Romance and adventure against the background of the War of 1812.

Hoffman, Peggy. *My dear cousin.* **Harcourt, 1970.**
A novel, based on real characters, of society in and around Baltimore in the period just before the War of 1812.

Hubbard, Lucien. *Rivers to the sea.* **Simon & Schuster, 1942.**
Action-packed story of a steamboat trip from Pittsburgh to New Orleans in 1811.

Jennings, John. *Salem frigate.* **Doubleday, 1946.**
Story of sea adventure and action against the Barbary pirates.

Jennings, John. *Tall ships.* **McGraw, 1958.**
Naval action in the period of the War of 1812.

Kane, Harnett. *Lady of Arlington.* Doubleday, 1953.
Biographical novel of Mary Custis Lee.

Kennelly, Ardyth. *Spur.* Messner, 1951.
An interpretation of the life and character of John Wilkes Booth.

Kent, Madeleine. *The corsair.* Doubleday, 1955.
Biographical novel of Jean Lafitte, pirate and companion of Jackson at the Battle of New Orleans.

Kroll, Harry. *Fury in the earth.* Bobbs, 1945.
A story of the earthquakes of 1811-12 that destroyed a river town on the Mississippi.

La Farge, Oliver. *Long pennant.* Houghton, 1933.
About the capture of a British ship by an American privateer in the War of 1812.

Laing, Alexander. *Jonathan Eagle.* Little, 1954.
A long, very well-written novel that portrays many aspects of American life around 1790 with vividness and thorough accuracy.

Laing, Alexander. *Matthew Early,* Duell, 1957.
Romance and adventure for a young New England sea captain who loves well if not wisely. Early 19th century.

Lancaster, Bruce. *For us, the living.* Stokes, 1940.
Early 19th century in Kentucky and Indiana, and the principal characters are two adolescent boys, one of whom is Abe Lincoln.

Lane, Carl. *Fleet in the forest.* Coward, 1943.
A novel about Perry's Lake Erie fleet and how it was built. Authentic material.

Lauritzen, Jonreed. *Everlasting fire.* Doubleday, 1962.
Story about the early trials and struggles of the Mormons in their westward migration from New York through the Middle West.

McNeilly, Mildred. *Heaven is too high.* Morrow, 1944.
About a Russian aristocrat who, threatened by the Empress Catherine, goes to Alaska and finds a new life there. Period: about 1800.

Miller, Heather R. *Gone a hundred miles.* Harcourt, 1968.
Good period piece set in the frontier of North Carolina in the early 1800's.

Muir, Robert. *Sprig of hemlock.* Longmans, 1957.
Story about a poor New England family who join with Captain Daniel Shays in his uprising on behalf of debtors in 1794.

Nelson, Truman. *Surveyor.* Doubleday, 1960.
Excellent long novel about John Brown, showing fully the impact he had on the slavery question in Kansas.

O'Neill, Charles. *Morning time.* Simon & Schuster, 1949.
Fast-moving and colorful novel of the years after the Revolution and of General Wilkinson's conspiracy.

Palmer, Bruce and Giles, John. *Horseshoe Bend.* Simon & Schuster, 1962.
Setting is Andrew Jackson's defeat of the Creek Indians in 1814. Story involves many famous persons and much action.

Parker, Cornelia. *Fabulous valley.* Putnam, 1956.
Romantic story involving the discovery of oil in Pennsylvania in 1859.

Roark, Garland. *Rainbow in the royals.* Doubleday, 1950.
Story of two brothers' voyage around the Horn to California in gold rush days. Good nautical details.

Roberts, Kenneth. *Captain Caution.* Doubleday, 1934.
Engrossing story of naval warfare in the War of 1812.

Roberts, Kenneth. *Lively Lady.* Doubleday, 1931.
In the War of 1812 an American naval captain is captured by the British and imprisoned on Dartmoor.

Roberts, Kenneth. *Lydia Bailey.* Doubleday, 1946.
An adventure story of many facets, ranging from Haiti during Toussaint's revolt to the wars of Tripoli.

Savage, Les. *Doniphan's ride.* Doubleday, 1959.
Story of a boy's experiences in the Mexican War.

Seifert, Shirley. *Turquoise trail.* Lippincott, 1950.
A fictionalized account of Susan Magoffin's journey from Missouri to Mexico during the Mexican War.

Seton, Anya. *My Theodosia.* Houghton, 1941.
Biographical novel about Theodosia, daughter of Aaron Burr, and a figure of romance and mystery.

Shepard, Odell and Willard. *Holdfast Gaines.* Macmillan, 1946.
Unusually good novel about an Indian raised by a white family during the period from the Revolution to the War of 1812.

Sperry, Armstrong. *No brighter glory.* Macmillan, 1942.
Romance and adventure in 1810, as Astor was building his fortune in the West and in New York.

Steward, Davenport. *Rainbow road.* Tupper, 1953.
About the men who, in the 1820's, converged on southern Georgia in search of gold.

Stone, Irving. *Love is eternal.* Doubleday, 1954.
About the marriage of Lincoln and Mary Todd. It is pictured as a true love match throughout, and Mrs. Lincoln as a kinder person than the usual portrait.

Stone, Irving. *The President's lady.* **Doubleday, 1951.**
Fictional account of the true romance of Andrew and Rachel Jackson.

Street, James. *Oh, promised land.* **Dial, 1940.**
A long graphic novel about the westward journey of a brother and sister from Georgia to the Mississippi between 1794 and 1817.

Taylor, Robert L. *Two roads to Guadalupe.* **Doubleday, 1964.**
An adventure story involving two American boys who join the Army to fight in the Mexican War. Colorful and full of action.

Teilhet, Darwin. *Steamboat on the river.* **Dutton, 1952.**
Story of a young man serving on the crew of a river boat on the Sangamon, in company with young Abe Lincoln.

Tracy, Don. *Crimson is the eastern shore.* **Dial, 1953.**
Full of blood and thunder, a novel about the War of 1812 on the Eastern Shore of Maryland.

Van Every, Dale. *Westward the river.* **Putnam, 1945.**
Action and romance on a flatboat journey down the Ohio in the 1790's.

Wallace, Willard M. *Jonathan Dearborn.* **Little, 1967.**
Novel centering around a young man's experiences in the War of 1812. Solid historical setting.

Waters, Gladys. *Fairacres.* **U. of Denver Pr., 1952.**
Describes realistically and sympathetically the pioneer founding of Independence, Missouri in 1826.

Wellman, Paul. *The Buckstones.* **Trident, 1967.**
Adventures of an indentured servant girl who goes from Tennessee to Washington, D. C., seeking aid from President Andrew Jackson for her imprisoned father.

West, Jessamyn. *Leafy rivers.* Harcourt, 1967.
Good re-creation of life in Ohio Territory about 1800. Pleasing heroine and local descriptions.

Wheelwright, Jere. *Kentucky stand.* Scribner, 1951.
A story about the settlement of the Old Southwest.

Wilson, William. *Abe Lincoln of Pigeon Creek.* McGraw, 1949.
Well-written novel of Lincoln's youth.

Wormser, Richard. *Battalion of saints.* McKay, 1960.
Story about a battalion of Mormons formed in Iowa who went to New Mexico to join in the Mexican War.

Wyckoff, Nicholas. *The Corinthians.* Macmillan, 1960.
Set in the Middle West in the mid-19th century, it is the story of a man with domestic problems, who is drawn into the orbit of the Mormon migration.

JUVENILE

Alderman, Clifford. *Wooden ships and iron men.* Walker, 1964.
Naval action in the War of 1812, in the form of a story about a young British sailor.

Andrews, Mary. *Lanterns aloft.* Longmans, 1955.
Story of two boys who help serve the American cause in the War of 1812 as British ships enter Chesapeake Bay.

Arntson, Herbert. *Adam Gray: stowaway.* Watts, 1961.
Adventure story of sailing ships in the early 19th century.

Aspden, Don. *Barney's barges.* Holiday, 1944.
Good story of the War of 1812 as it was seen by boatmen trying to defend the Chesapeake from the British.

Best, Herbert. *Watergate.* **Winston, 1951.**
Story for boys about the Irish who worked on the Erie Canal in its early days.

Boyd, Marion. *Strange island.* **World, 1957.**
Good story about a governess to the Blennerhassett family who became so closely involved in Aaron Burr's mysterious plot to acquire a western empire for himself.

Brett, Grace. *The runaway.* **Follett, 1958.**
Story about a young boy in the Carolinas in the early 1800's. He learns he is not really the son of the man who is cruel to him, but actually a shipwreck castaway. He runs away to search for his own parents.

Brown, J. D. *The freeholder.* **Morrow, 1949.**
About an English orphan boy who comes to America as an indentured servant in the early 19th century.

Butler, Beverly. *Silver key.* **Dodd, 1961.**
Girls' story about a girl and her family in a new home in Wisconsin just before the Civil War. Mystery, romance, and good authentic background on fugitive slaves.

Carr, Harriett. *Wheels for conquest.* **Macmillan, 1957.**
About two boys' adventures in the early days of western Pennsylvania, centering around the fur trade and building of Conestoga wagons.

Cavanah, Frances. *Two loves for Jenny Lind.* **Macrae Smith, 1956.**
Biographical novel about the Swedish singer, and especially her American visit in 1850.

Dahl, Borghild. *Stowaway to America.* **Dutton, 1959.**
Story of a Norwegian girl who stows away on a ship carrying a group of Norwegians planning to found a colony in New York State in 1825. Based on fact, with good background.

Davis, Julia. *Ride with the eagle.* **Harcourt, 1962.**
Based on diaries kept by six soldiers in an American regiment in the Mexican War, this is the story of their battles under Colonel Doniphan.

Dean, Leon. *Guns over Champlain.* **Rinehart, 1946.**
Exciting story of a boy's adventures during the War of 1812 in the action on and around Lake Champlain.

Du Soe, Robert. *Boatswain's boy.* **Longmans, 1950.**
Good seafaring adventure story of the War of 1812.

Du Soe, Robert. *Detached command.* **Longmans, 1954.**
Deals with American naval life around 1815.

Du Soe, Robert. *Your orders, sir.* **Longmans, 1953.**
Story of the Chesapeake Bay blockade in the War of 1812.

Eifert, Virginia. *Out of the wilderness.* **Dodd, 1956.**
Well-written novel about Lincoln in his teen-age years, when his family was moving from Kentucky to Illinois.

Eifert, Virginia. *Three rivers south.* **Dodd, 1953.**
Story about the young Abe Lincoln's flatboat journey down the Mississippi to New Orleans.

Emery, Anne. *Spy in old New Orleans.* **Rand McNally, 1960.**
Story about a boy who fights with Jean Lafitte in the Battle of New Orleans in 1815.

Evernden, Margery. *Wilderness boy.* **Putnam, 1955.**
Good story dealing with the Whiskey Rebellion of 1794.

Finger, Charles J. *When guns thundered at Tripoli.* **Holt, 1937.**
Exciting story of a ship's boy from New England who is captured by pirates on the Barbary Coast and takes part in the naval fighting there.

Fisher, Aileen. *My cousin Abe.* **Nelson, 1962.**
Fictionalized story of young Lincoln, purportedly by Dennis Hanks.

Grant, Bruce. *Eagle of the sea.* **Rand McNally, 1949.**
Fictionalized account of the exploits of the *USS Constitution* with two real-life boys as centers of interest.

Howard, Elizabeth. *Candle in the night.* **Morrow, 1952.**
Love and adventure in a story of the West and especially of Detroit in the War of 1812.

Howard, Elizabeth. *North winds blow free.* **Morrow, 1949.**
Romantic novel about a girl in northern Michigan in the 1850's who helps runaway slaves escaping to Canada.

Hungerford, Edward. *Forbidden island.* **Wilcox & Follett, 1950.**
Colorful story for boys about Commodore Perry's expedition to Japan in 1853.

Hunt, Mabel L. *Better known as Johnny Appleseed.* **Lippincott, 1950.**
Interesting account, well illustrated, of the story of John Chapman, one of the true legends of the middle west.

Jackson, Phyllis. *Victorian Cinderella.* **Holiday, 1947.**
Fictionalized biography of Harriet Beecher Stowe.

Kohler, J. H. *Harmony ahead.* **Aladdin, 1952.**
Story about the settlement of New Harmony, Indiana, the communal experiment of Robert Owen.

Koob, Theodora. *Surgeon's apprentice.* **Lippincott, 1963.**
Set in Virginia in the early 19th century, this relates the experiences of a boy who becomes apprentice to his father, a physician.

Kummer, Frederic. *For flag and freedom.* **Morrow, 1942.**
A teen-age boy takes part in 1812 in the fighting around Baltimore, including the defense of Fort McHenry.

Longstreth, Thomas. *Hide-out.* Macmillan, 1947.
About a boy living in Concord in the 1840's when railroads were ousting stagecoaches, and great literary figures were neighbors.

Lowe, Corinne. *Quicksilver Bob.* Harcourt, 1946.
Fictionalized life of Robert Fulton, builder of the *Clermont.*

Masters, Kelly. *Keelboat journey.* Dutton, 1958.
A boy joins the crew of a keelboat in a race up the Missouri in the 1830's. Good background.

Meader, Stephen. *Voyage of the Javelin.* Harcourt, 1959.
A teen-age boy's adventures on a round-the-world voyage of a 19th century clipper ship.

Meader, Stephen. *Whaler 'round the Horn.* Harcourt, 1950.
Story about a boy on a New Bedford whaling ship in the mid-19th century.

Meadowcroft, Enid. *By secret railway.* Crowell, 1948.
Story about the assistance given to escaping slaves before the Civil War.

Nolan, Jeannette. *Patriot in the saddle.* Messner, 1945.
Adventure and mystery; story of a boy raised in the woods of Tennessee in the early 1800's. He becomes of service to Madison and Jackson.

O'Connor, Patrick. *Flight of the Peacock.* Washburn, 1954.
Boys' adventure story about the China clippers.

Parks, Edd. *Little Long Rifle.* Bobbs, 1949.
A boy's story in frontier Tennessee in 1801, when Spaniards and horse thieves were natural enemies.

Person, Tom. *Trouble on the trace.* Ariel, 1954.
Adventure on the Natchez Trace at the beginning of the 19th century.

Robertson, Keith. *Ice to India.* **Viking, 1955.**
Good story of a boy's experiences on a clipper ship from Philadelphia to Calcutta.

Sperry, Armstrong. *Black falcon.* **Winston, 1949.**
Exciting story of a boy's experiences in the Battle of New Orleans. Jackson and Lafitee are leading figures.

Sperry, Armstrong. *Storm canvas.* **Winston, 1944.**
Plenty of action in this story of the naval phase of the War of 1812 and of the court of Henri Christophe of Haiti.

Sterne, Emma. *Long black schooner.* **Aladdin, 1953.**
Story based on the actual revolt of a cargo of slaves from Africa in 1839.

Swanson, Neil and Anne. *Star spangled banner.* **Winston, 1958.**
Story about a boy involved in the attack on Fort McHenry in the War of 1812.

Tufts, Anne. *Rails along the Chesapeake.* **Holt, 1957.**
Set partly in Massachusetts and partly in Baltimore, this story deals with the building of the first American locomotive in 1830.

Webb, Christopher. *Quest of the Otter.* **Funk, 1963.**
Exciting story of a whaling ship in the middle 1800's.

Williamson, Joanne. *Glorious conspiracy.* **Knopf, 1961.**
A boy who has grown up in the slums of industry in early 19th century England, comes to America and becomes involved in the political ideas and rivalries of that day.

THE CIVIL WAR PERIOD

Allen, Henry. *Journey to Shiloh.* **Random, 1960.**
The experiences of seven young men who are taken into the Confederate Army and fight at Corinth and Shiloh.

Allen, Hervey. *Action at Aquila.* **Farrar, 1938.**
Superior novel about the Civil War in the Shenandoah Valley in 1864.

Appell, George C. *The man who shot Quantrill.* **Doubleday, 1957.**
Fast action about a Union detachment in pursuit of the Confederate raiders under Quantrill.

Barney, Helen. *Green rose of Furley.* **Crown, 1953.**
Romantic story of a Quaker girl whose father's farm was a refuge for escaping slaves during the Civil War.

Becker, Stephen. *When the war is over.* **Random, 1969.**
An unusual story of the Civil War, in which a young orphaned Kentucky boy wounds a Union lieutenant. Their subsequent friendship helps them through the ugliness and squalor of the war.

Borland, Hal G. *The amulet.* **Lippincott, 1957.**
The Civil War as it came to people on the Great Plains and in Missouri.

Boyd, James. *Marching on.* **Scribner, 1927.**
Good Civil War story. The hero is a Southern soldier from the small farmer class. Gives an unusual view-point of the war.

Branson, H. C. *Salisbury Plain.* **Dutton, 1965.**
Civil War novel with an imaginary setting in Virginia, and an analogy between the Union general and King Arthur.

Brick, John. *Jubilee.* **Doubleday, 1956.**
A stirring Civil War novel, with special focus on Sherman's march.

Brick, John. *Troubled spring.* **Farrar, 1950.**
A Union veteran returns from Andersonville Prison after the Civil War to his Hudson River village to find that many things have changed, not for the best.

Brier, Royce. *Boy in blue.* **Appleton, 1937.**
Story about an ordinary Union soldier's experiences fighting in the Cumberland Valley and the Battle of Chickamauga.

Cain, James. *Mignon.* **Dial, 1962.**
Lusty story of New Orleans near the close of the Civil War.

Carrighar, Sally. *The glass dove.* **Doubleday, 1961.**
A young woman lives with her father on an Ohio farm that was a "station" for runaway slaves. During the Civil War she runs it alone and falls in love with a wounded soldier.

Churchill, Winston. *The crisis.* **Macmillan, 1901.**
Old but classic novel of the clash of rival groups in Missouri during the Civil War.

Corrington, John W. *And wait for the night.* **Putnam, 1964.**
A long, well-written novel of the last days of the Civil War, and the Union occupation of Louisiana. Pro-Southern point-of-view.

Crabbs, Alfred. *Home to Tennessee.* **Bobbs, 1952.**
A strongly realistic novel of the Civil War in Tennessee.

Crabb, Alfred. *A mockingbird sang at Chickamauga.* **Bobbs, 1949.**
Interesting story of the Civil War around Chattanooga in 1863.

Crane, Stephen. *Red badge of courage.* **Appleton, 1895.**
Literary classic of realism. Battle of Chancellorsville as experienced by a young Union soldier.

Delmar, Vina. *Beloved.* **Harcourt, 1956.**
Fictionalized and romantic biography of Judah P. Benjamin, one of the leading figures of the Confederacy.

Demarest, Phyllis. *Wilderness brigade.* **Doubleday, 1956.**
A Union soldier escapes from a Confederate prison, and is sheltered by a Southern family, in whose lives he becomes closely involved.

Dowdey, Clifford. *Bugles blow no more.* **Little, 1937.**
A novel of Richmond during the Civil War. The details of the setting are authentic and fascinating.

Dowdey, Clifford. *Proud retreat.* **Doubleday, 1953.**
A story of the Confederate effort to save its treasury in the evacuation of Richmond near the end of the war.

Eberhart, Mignon G. *The cup, the blade or the gun.* **Random, 1961.**
Romantic mystery and adventure about a New England girl who marries a Confederate officer during the Civil War.

Fast, Howard. *Freedom road.* **Duell, 1944.**
A novel of the early Reconstruction days in the South, when Negroes had many political opportunities. An important picture of the period, though strongly anti-white.

Feuille, Frank. *Cotton road.* **Morrow, 1954.**
Based on fact, this tells how two young men during the Civil War took a wagon train of cotton to a coastal point where the northern blockade was weak.

Foote, Shelby. *Shiloh.* **Dial, 1952.**
Vivid account of the battle, and how it affected several participants.

Glasgow, Ellen. *Battle-ground.* **Doubleday, 1920.**
Picture of a Virginia plantation before and during the Civil War, reflecting the effects of the conflict.

Haas, Ben. *The foragers.* **Simon & Schuster, 1962.**
Fast-paced story of a southern plantation family and a troop of Confederates looking for supplies — a mutual struggle for survival in wartime.

Hart, Scott. *Eight April days.* **Coward, 1949.**
Vivid and well-told account of the retreat of Confederate forces from Petersburg to Appomattox.

Hebson, Ann. *The Lattimer legend.* **Macmillan, 1961.**
The Civil War in West Virginia as reflected in the diaries of a woman
with Morgan's raiders.

Horan, James. *Seek out and destroy.* **Crown, 1958.**
Story of a Confederate naval vessel which makes a voyage half way
round the world in an attempt to destroy Northern whaling fleets.

Johnston, Mary. *The long roll.* **Houghton, 1911.**
Story chiefly about the career of Stonewall Jackson in the Civil War.

Kane, Harnett. *Gallant Mrs. Stonewall.* **Doubleday, 1957.**
Tells of the Civil War as seen and experienced by General Jackson's
second wife.

Kane, Harnett. *Smiling rebel.* **Doubleday, 1955.**
Civil War story about the Confederate spy, Belle Boyd.

Kantor, MacKinlay. *Andersonville.* **World, 1955.**
Extremely long, vivid and starkly real novel centering about life in
and around the Confederate prison at Andersonville, Georgia.

Kantor, MacKinlay. *Arouse and beware.* **Coward, 1936.**
A gripping and realistic Civil War story, about the escape of two
Union soldiers from the Confederate prison of Belle Island and their
desperate journey toward safety.

Kantor, MacKinlay. *Long remember.* **Coward, 1934.**
Vivid picture of the Battle of Gettysburg as seen by a local resident.

Keyes, Frances P. *The chess players.* **Farrar, 1960.**
Long novel of romance and glamor in New Orleans and Paris in the
mid-1800's. The central figure is world's chess champion Paul
Morphy.

Lancaster, Bruce. *No bugles tonight.* **Little, 1948.**
Good Civil War story about a Northern officer acting as a secret
agent in Tennessee, and his romance with a Southern widow.

Lancaster, Bruce. *Roll, Shenandoah.* **Little, 1956.**
Sound and realistic portrayal of General Sheridan's activities in
Virginia during the Civil War.

Lancaster, Bruce. *Scarlet patch.* **Little, 1947.**
Good Civil War novel concerning the foreign-born volunteers in the
Union Army.

Lancaster, Bruce and Brentano, Lowell. *Bride of a thousand cedars.*
Stokes, 1939.
A novel about the various effects on the people of Bermuda of the
Civil War blockade-running activities there.

Le May, Alan. *By dim and flaring lamps.* **Harper, 1962.**
Vivid story set in Missouri at the time of the Civil War, when the
state was the stage for many rival factions.

Lentz, Perry. *Falling hills.* **Scribner, 1967.**
Centers around the Fort Pillow massacre in the Civil War, in which
Confederate troops attacked a Union fort in Tennessee, occupied by
Negro troops, and killed most of them.

Longstreet, Stephen. *Gettysburg.* **Farrar, 1961.**
Story about the people who lived in the town during the battle, and
how ordinary life still goes on in times of crisis.

Love, Edmund G. *A shipment of tarts.* **Doubleday, 1967.**
Humorous and action-filled Civil War novel, involving the harrassed
efforts of a young Union officer to carry out his orders to rid
Memphis of prostitutes and convey them up the Mississippi to Cairo,
Illinois.

Mason, Van Wyck. *Blue hurricane.* **Lippincott, 1954.**
A novel loaded with action and melodrama about naval warfare on the western rivers during the Civil War.

Mason, Van Wyck. *Our valiant few.* **Little, 1956.**
Action and melodrama along the Southern coast as the Confederates try to break the Union blockade.

Mason, Van Wyck. *Proud new flags.* **Lippincott, 1951.**
The Confederate navy in the first years of the Civil War is the principal and well-described subject of this novel.

McMeekin, Clark. *Tyrone of Kentucky.* **Appleton, 1954.**
About a Confederate soldier who returns to his Kentucky farm after the War, and tries to restore it during the conflicts of Reconstruction.

Miller, Helen T. *After the glory.* **Appleton, 1958.**
Story of a Tennessee family, divided by the Civil War, as it copes with problems of reconstruction days.

Miller, Helen T. and Topping, John. *Rebellion road.* **Bobbs, 1954.**
Story of a Confederate veteran's struggle to farm his Alabama land after the war. Good background.

Mitchell, Margaret. *Gone with the wind.* **Macmillan, 1936.**
Famous novel of the effects of the Civil War and Reconstruction on the life of a Georgia plantation and its people.

Morrison, Gerry. *Unvexed to the sea.* **St. Martins, 1960.**
A Civil War novel set around the siege of Vicksburg and Sherman's march to the sea.

Perenyi, Eleanor. *Bright sword.* **Rinehart, 1955.**
Good Civil War story written around the career of the Confederate General John Hood.

Rhodes, James and Jauchius, Dean. *Johnny Shiloh*. Bobbs, 1959.
Good novel about Johnny Shiloh who fought throughout the Civil War, the youngest soldier of all.

Robertson, Constance. *Golden Circle*. Random, 1953.
Fast-moving and realistic novel of the Civil War, dealing especially with Vallandigham and the "copperheads" and anti-government activity in Ohio.

Robertson, Constance. *The unterrified*. Holt, 1946.
Good story of an important New York State family during the Civil War, sharply divided in its attitudes toward the conflict.

Robertson, Don. *By Antietam Creek*. Prentice, 1960.
The bloody Antietam fighting graphically described.

Robertson, Don. *The three days*. Prentice, 1959.
A vivid novel of the Battle of Gettysburg, as it was seen by a few participants.

Schaefer, Jack. *Company of cowards*. Houghton, 1957.
Story of how a company of Union soldiers, discredited by previous cowardice, win back their self-respect and reputations.

Seifert, Shirley. *Farewell, my general*. Lippincott, 1954.
Novel about the career of Confederate general Jeb Stuart.

Seifert, Shirley. *The Senator's lady*. Lippincott, 1967.
About Mrs. Stephen A. Douglas. Good historical background and authentic material.

Sims, Marian. *Beyond surrender*. Lippincott, 1942.
Story of a Confederate officer's experiences in his community in Reconstruction days.

Sinclair, Harold. *Horse soldiers.* **Harper, 1955.**
Realistic and vividly-told account, in fictional form, of the Civil War
incident called Grierson's Raid.

Slaughter, Frank G. *Lorena.* **Doubleday, 1959.**
Story of a southern woman who had to manage a plantation during
and after the Civil War.

Stacton, David. *Judges of the secret court.* **Pantheon, 1961.**
Biographical novel about John Wilkes Booth, chiefly during the two
weeks between Lincoln's assassination and Booth's own death in a
Virginia barn.

Stern, Philip V. *Drums of morning.* **Doubleday, 1942.**
Good novel covering the American scene from 1837 to 1865, showing,
through the career of one person, the basic causes of the Civil War.

Street, James. *By valour and arms.* **Dial, 1944.**
Long and vigorous Civil War novel, from the Southern viewpoint.
Deals particularly with naval warfare on the Mississippi.

Toepfer, Ray. *Scarlet guidon.* **Coward, 1958.**
Story about a group of Alabamans serving in the same company in
the Civil War, and what happened to each one.

Tracy, Don. *On the midnight tide.* **Dial, 1957.**
About Confederate blockade runners. Action and romance.

Wagner, Constance. *Ask my brother.* **Harper, 1958.**
Set in Chambersburg, Pennsylvania, at the time of the Civil War. A
story of a marriage of a Southern woman and a Northern husband.

Wallace, Willard. *The raiders.* **Little, 1970.**
A novel of the Civil War, told in the first person. The narrator
is a Union naval officer, and the ravages of the Confederate ship
Alabama comprise only part of the action.

Warren, Robert Penn. *Wilderness.* **Random, 1961.**
Philosophical novel of a Bavarian Jew who comes to America during
the Civil War in a search for the meaning of freedom.

Weekley, Robert. *House in ruins.* **Random, 1958.**
A group of former Confederate soldiers carry on guerrilla warfare
against Union troops occupying their Mississippi town after the
Civil War.

Wellman, Manly. *Ghost battalion.* **Washburn, 1958.**
A young Confederate joins a group of saboteurs behind Union lines
and finds high adventure.

Wheelwright, Jere. *Gray captain.* **Scribner, 1954.**
Well-done account of a Confederate infantry company in Northern
Virginia in 1864, as the shadow of defeat fell on the South.

Williams, Ben Ames. *House divided.* **Houghton, 1947.**
This extremely long novel is a panorama of the Civil War, particularly seen through southern eyes.

Wilson, William E. *The raiders.* **Rinehart, 1955.**
Story of the drama of an Ohio border town in the Civil War when it
is attacked by Morgan's raiders.

Yerby, Frank. *Captain rebel.* **Dial, 1956.**
A story of Confederate blockade running, with more romance and
melodrama than history.

Yerby, Frank. *The vixens.* **Dial, 1947.**
Reconstruction politics and violence in New Orleans after the Civil
War.

Young, Stark. *So red the rose.* **Scribner, 1934.**
Very popular novel of life in Mississippi before and during the
Civil War.

Zara, Louis. *Rebel run.* **Crown, 1951.**
An account, in graphic terms, of the Andrews Raid in 1862, when a group of Federal soldiers tried to cut railway transportation between Chattanooga and Atlanta.

JUVENILE

Abrahams, Robert. *Mr. Benjamin's sword.* **Jewish Publ., 1948.**
Story of Judah P. Benjamin's escape to England after the Civil War.

Allen, Merritt. *Blow, bugles, blow.* **Longmans, 1956.**
Very colorful story of Sheridan's forces toward the end of the Civil War.

Allen, Merritt. *Johnny Reb.* **Longmans, 1952.**
A good picture of the Civil War as seen by a boy serving with General Wade Hampton's Confederate troops.

Allen, Merritt. *White feather.* **Longmans, 1944.**
Story of a Kentucky mountain boy who fights with Morgan's raiders in the Civil War, and changes his grandfather's poor opinion of him.

Brick, John. *Yankees on the run.* **Duell, 1961.**
Story of how two Union soldiers escaped from Andersonville Prison.

Edmonds, Walter D. *Cadmus Henry.* **Dodd, 1949.**
Enjoyable Civil War story about a boy who becomes a balloonist for the Confederates.

Eifert, Virginia. *New birth of freedom.* **Dodd, 1959.**
Last of five volumes of a fictionalized life of Lincoln. Well-done.

Hinkins, Virginia. *Stonewall's courier.* **McGraw, 1959.**
Based on fact, ths is the story of a Virginia boy who became a courier for General Jackson in the Shenandoah.

Hunt, Irene. *Across five Aprils*. Follett, 1964.
Warm story of a young boy who must take the responsibility for his father's Illinois farm during the Civil War.

Keith, Harold. *Rifles for Watie*. Crowell, 1957.
Exciting story about Cherokee raids on Union troops in the West during the Civil War.

McGiffen, Lee. *Coat for Private Patrick*. Dutton, 1964.
Story of the Civil War, in which a young Southerner becomes a telegrapher.

Meader, Stephen. *Muddy road to glory*. Harcourt, 1963.
Story of a Maine boy's experiences in the Civil War.

Miers, Earl S. *Guns of Vicksburg*. Putnam, 1957.
Adventures of a young Union spy inside Vicksburg during the siege.

Norton, Andre. *Ride proud, rebel!* World, 1961.
A boy rides as a scout with Morgan's raiders, the famous Confederate band of guerrilla fighters.

Sayre, Anne. *Never call retreat*. Crowell, 1957.
A teen-age girl and her Quaker family become involved in Reconstruction days in Alabama.

Steele, William. *Perilous road*. Harcourt, 1958.
A boy learns the problems of divided loyalties in his Tennessee home during the Civil War.

White, Dale. *Steamboat up the Missouri*. Viking, 1958.
Good description of river boats in Civil War days.

Whitney, Phyllis. *Step to the music*. Crowell, 1953.
Deals with the New York City draft riots during the Civil War.

177

1876-1916

Carse, Robert. *Beckoning waters.* **Scribner, 1953.**
Story of an immigrant's career on the Great Lakes, where he rises to become a shipping tycoon. Period from 1876 to 1932.

Castor, Henry. *Year of the Spaniard.* **Doubleday, 1950.**
Story of two Philadelphia college boys' participation in the war with Spain in Cuba in 1898.

Cookson, Catherine. *Katie Mulholland.* **Bobbs, 1967.**
Romantic melodrama covering eighty years of a woman's eventful life, from 1860 to the Second World War.

Davis, Clyde Brion. *Jeremy Bell.* **Rinehart, 1947.**
Story about two Northern farm boys who, about 1898, become workers in a wretched Southern lumber camp. Escaping from this, they join the army in the war against Spain.

Fast, Howard. *The American.* **Duell, 1946.**
A biographical novel about John Peter Altgeld, the liberal Illinois governor in the 1890's. Strongly sympathetic.

Ferber, Edna. *Saratoga trunk.* **Doubleday, 1941.**
Fascinating characters in the milieu of racehorses, multi-millionaries and high society in the late 19th century.

Idell, Albert. *Bridge to Brooklyn.* **Holt, 1944.**
A sequel to *Centennial Summer*. The Rogers family has moved to Brooklyn around 1883, when the famous bridge was completed. Enjoyable characters and plenty of nostalgia.

Idell, Albert. *Centennial summer.* **Holt, 1943.**
Pleasant story about an interesting Philadelphia family in 1876, the centennial year.

Idell, Albert. *Great blizzard.* **Holt, 1948.**
Tells of the enjoyable Rogers family in New York City in the 1880's, especially during the great storm of 1888.

O'Connor, Richard. *Officers and ladies.* **Doubleday, 1958.**
Story of two dissimilar brothers serving in the American occupation forces in the Philippines at the turn of the century.

Robertson, Don. *Paradise Falls.* **Putnam, 1968.**
Very long and panoramic novel of people in a southern Ohio town in the late 19th century.

Stevenson, Janet. *Ardent years.* **Viking, 1960.**
Fictionalized biography of the actress Fanny Kemble and particularly of her marriage with a wealthy Georgia planter.

Stewart, Ramona. *Casey.* **Little, 1968.**
The career of an Irish gangfighter who climbs to become boss of New York City in the mid-19th century. Strong local color.

Tarkington, Booth. *Magnificent Ambersons.* **Doubleday, 1918.**
Novel of a mid-western family of the 1870's.

Tebbel, John. *Voice in the streets.* **Dutton, 1954.**
Story of a man's rise to power in New York City in mid-19th century. Good background.

JUVENILE

Bell, Margaret. *Watch for a tall white sail.* **Morrow, 1948.**
Excellent story for high school girls, set in the hardships of a family's experiences in Alaska in 1887.

Friermood, Elisabeth. *Doc Dudley's daughter.* **Doubleday, 1965.**
Period of the Spanish-American War set in a small town.

Havighurst, Walter, and Boyd, Marion. *Climb a lofty ladder*. Winston, 1952.
Story about Swedish farmers in Minnesota in the 1890's.

Oakes, Virginia. *Desert harvest*. Winston, 1952.
Story depicting Japanese settlement in the farm lands of California.

Smith, Frederika. *Fire dragon*. Rand, McNally, 1956.
Two boys and the great fire of Chicago in 1871.

Wibberley, Leonard. *Wound of Peter Wayne*. Farrar, 1955.
Good story of a young Southerner who goes west to seek his fortune after the Civil War.

WORLD WAR I TO 1941

Bellow, Saul. *Adventures of Augie March*. Viking, 1953.
Lower class life in Chicago in the 1920's.

Binns, Archie. *Laurels are cut down*. Reynal, 1937.
Deals mainly with the American campaign in Siberia after World War I.

Boyd, Thomas. *Through the wheat*. Scribner, 1923.
Excellent characterization of an ordinary soldier in World War I.

Campbell, William. *Company K*. Random, 1933.
Good picture of a single company's experiences in the First World War, told in a series of sketches and episodes about individual members.

Daniels, Guy. *Progress, U.S.A*. Macmillan, 1968.
Teen-age boy in a small American town of the 1930's. Enjoyable characterizations of people of a period that seems long ago.

Dutton, Mary. *Thorpe.* World, 1967.
Life and problems in a small Arkansas town in the 1930's, as observed through the eyes of a six-year-old girl.

Hemingway, Ernest. *Farewell to arms.* Scribner, 1929.
Noted romantic novel of an American soldier on the Italian front in World War I.

Nason, Leonard. *Chevrons.* Doran, 1926.
Enjoyable and popular account of army life during the First World War.

Powell, Richard. *I take this land.* Scribner, 1962.
Melodrama about the development of southern Florida around the turn of the century.

Smith, Betty. *A tree grows in Brooklyn.* Harper, 1943.
Excellent novel about a poor city family during the World War I era.

Steinbeck, John. *Grapes of wrath.* Viking, 1939.
Famous story of a family of "Okies" who, during the great dust storms of the 1930's, leave their ruined farm in the Plains and migrate to California.

Weaver, John. *Another such victory.* Viking, 1948.
Story of a family who in the summer of 1932 lived among the Bonus Army veterans in Washington.

JUVENILE

Clarke, Tom. *Big road.* Lothrop, 1965.
Trials of a jobless young man in the days of the 1930's depression.

WORLD WAR II AND AFTER

Beach, Edward L. *Run silent, run deep*. Holt, 1955.
An exciting and highly authentic novel about a submarine patrol in the Pacific during World War II.

Brown, Harry. *Walk in the sun*. Knopf, 1944.
A contemporary novel of unusual quality about a squad of American soldiers in Italy during World War II.

Chamales, Tom. *Never so few*. Scribner, 1957.
Story of guerrilla warfare in Burma in World War II.

Charyn, Jerome. *American scrapbook*. Viking, 1969.
The harsh experiences of six members of a Japanese-American family interned in California during World War II.

Clagett, John. *The slot*. Crown, 1958.
Story about American naval action around Guadalcanal and the Solomons in World War II.

Dibner, Martin. *Deep six*. Doubleday, 1953.
Naval story of World War II.

Dodson, Kenneth. *Away all boats*. Little, 1954.
Amphibious warfare in the Pacific during World War II.

Flood, Charles B. *More lives than one*. Houghton, 1967.
The story of an American captive in a Korean Communist prison-camp, and of the romantic problems he faces after his release.

Forester, C. S. *Good shepherd*. Little, 1955.
Novel about a merchant ship convoy and its escort to England during World War II, told by a master of naval action.

182

Heller, Joseph. *Catch-22.* Simon & Schuster, 1961.
One of the outstanding comic and satiric novels of the Second World War.

Hersey, John. *Bell for Adano.* Knopf, 1944.
Excellent novel about an American officer in charge of governing a small Italian town during the occupation, and of his problems in coping with local customs and fascist habits.

Hersey, John. *The war lover.* Knopf, 1959.
Realistic account of the daily doings of an American Flying Fortress crew in England in World War II.

Jones, James. *From here to eternity.* Scribner, 1951.
Highly realistic and adult novel depicting army life in Hawaii just prior to and including the attack on Pearl Harbor.

Jones, James. *Thin red line.* Scribner, 1962.
Story of a rifle company on Guadalcanal. Realistic action and language.

Lamott, Kenneth. *The stockade.* Little, 1952.
About an American prison camp on a Pacific island, in which 5000 Okinawans and Koreans were imprisoned during World War II.

Landon, Joseph. *Angle of attack.* Doubleday, 1952.
Realistic novel about an air bomber crew in World War II.

Loomis, Edward. *End of a war.* Ballantine, 1957.
Novel about the experiences and reactions of an infantryman during the last years of World War II in Western Europe.

MacCuish, David. *Do not go gentle.* Doubleday, 1960.
A World War II story of a young man in the Marine Corps.

Mailer, Norman. *Naked and the dead.* **Rinehart, 1948.**
A graphic and realistic picture of the effects of war on men; story of the capture of a Japanese island by marines in World War II.

Shapiro, Lionel. *Sixth of June.* **Doubleday, 1955.**
American invasion of Normandy, with excellent wartime background and a romantic plot.

Taylor, Ward. *Roll back the sky.* **Holt, 1956.**
Deals with the men who flew bombing missions over Japan in World War II.

Uris, Leon. *Battle cry.* **Putnam, 1953.**
Exciting story of Marine action during World War II.

Van Praag, V. *Day without end.* **Sloane, 1949.**
Very graphic picture of one day in the life of a platoon in the Normandy invasion.

White, Theodore. *Mountain road.* **Sloane, 1958.**
Realistic and challenging novel about an American officer's job in 1944 of evacuating his own as well as Chinese forces from Liuchow in the face of advancing Japanese.

Wouk, Herman. *Caine mutiny.* **Doubleday, 1951.**
One of the most highly regarded stories of naval life and action.

JUVENILE

Norton, Andre. *Sword in sheath.* **Harcourt, 1949.**
A thriller about two young Americans who, just after the Second War, are commissioned to go to the East Indies to trace an American flyer lost there.

THE WEST

Ainsworth, Edward. *Eagles fly west.* **Macmillan, 1946.**
Novel about the settlement of California and its development into statehood. Colorful and authentic.

Allen, T. D. *Troubled border.* **Harper, 1954.**
A good novel about the early settlement of the Pacific Northwest, and particularly about the chief factor of the Hudson's Bay Company, John McLoughlin.

Arnold, Elliot. *Blood brother.* **Duell, 1947.**
Story about the Apache wars in the old Southwest.

Baker, Karle. *Star of the wilderness.* **Coward, 1942.**
Story of pioneers settling in Texas while it was still Mexican territory.

Barrett, Monte. *Tempered blade.* **Bobbs, 1946.**
Novel about Jim Bowie, frontiersman who died at the Alamo.

Bean, Amelia. *Fancher train.* **Doubleday, 1958.**
Fictionalized account of the Mountain Meadows massacre, in which some 120 pioneers were murdered passing through Utah in 1857.

Bean, Amelia. *The feud.* **Doubleday, 1960.**
A two-fisted gun war that actually occurred in Arizona in the 1880's.

Bean, Amelia. *Time for outrage.* **Doubleday, 1967.**
Story of lawlessness and political corruption in New Mexico Territory in the 1870's.

Berry, Don. *Moontrap.* **Viking, 1962.**
Set in Oregon in 1850, an excellent novel of pioneer violence and courage as exemplified by two mountain men.

Berry, Don. *To build a ship.* **Viking, 1963.**
A group of settlers on the Oregon coast in the 1850's undertake to build a ship, and the enterprise dominates everyone's life.

Berry, Don. *Trask.* **Viking, 1960.**
The early settlers of Oregon in the 1840's and the hardships they faced.

Binns, Archie. *Land is bright.* **Scribner, 1939.**
Good novel of the migration of a family from Illinois to Oregon in the 1850's.

Binns, Archie. *Yon rolling river.* **Scribner, 1947.**
Early pioneer days around Fort Astoria in the Columbia River region.

Birney, Hoffman. *Eagle in the sun.* **Putnam, 1935.**
Vivid novel of the Mexican War in the Southwest.

Birney, Hoffman. *Grim journey.* **Minton, 1934.**
Absorbing novel of the Donner Party tragedy, based entirely on fact and real people.

Blackburn, Thomas. *A good day to die.* **McKay, 1967.**
Deals with the last stand of Sitting Bull and the Sioux in 1890. Graphic story.

Blacker, Irwin. *Taos.* **World, 1959.**
Long and very vivid novel about the revolt of the Pueblo Indians against Spanish domination in 1680. Realistic and authentic.

Blake, Forrester. *Johnny Christmas.* **Morrow, 1948.**
Americans contend with Mexicans and Indians in Texas during the 1830's and 1840's.

Blake, Forrester. *Wilderness passage.* **Random, 1952.**
Good novel about the conflict between the Mormons and the United States Army in Utah's early days.

Borland, Hal. *Seventh winter.* **Lippincott, 1960.**
Story of a bitter winter in the old cattle country, told with realistic force.

Bosworth, Jim. *Long way north.* **Doubleday, 1959.**
Authentic and realistic account of a cattle drive from Texas to Montana Territory. Plot is slight, but action powerful.

Boyd, James. *Bitter creek.* **Scribner, 1939.**
Realistic story of experiences encountered by a runaway boy in the Far West of the 1880's.

Brown, Dee. *Wave high the banner.* **Macrae Smith, 1942.**
Story of Davy Crockett and the Texan revolution.

Burgess, Jackson. *Pillar of cloud.* **Putnam, 1957.**
Trail-blazing by a group of pioneers from Kansas to the Rockies in 1858.

Burnett, William. *Adobe walls.* **Knopf, 1953.**
Exciting western about the last uprising of the Apaches.

Burnett, William. *Mi amigo.* **Knopf, 1959.**
About Billy the Kid and range wars in New Mexico in the 1870's.

Capps, Benjamin. *The trail to Ogallala.* **Duell, 1964.**
Novel about a cattle drive from Texas to Nebraska, told with realism and historical authority.

Cather, Willa. *Death comes for the archbishop.* **Knopf, 1927.**
Excellent novel of the early days of New Mexico.

187

Caudill, Harry M. *Dark hills to westward.* **Little, 1969.**
This is the true story, in fiction form, of Jennie Wiley, a young woman of frontier Virginia who, in 1789, was carried off by Indians and held captive for a year.

Clark, Walter. *Ox-bow incident.* **Random, 1940.**
One of the most highly regarded novels of the Western genre. It deals with one day in the 1880's and with a lynching.

Cohen, Octavus R. *Borrasca.* **Macmillan, 1953.**
Story of prospecting and the Comstock Lode in the 1870's.

Constant, Alberta. *Oklahoma run.* **Crowell, 1955**
Set in the dramatic events of the opening of Oklahoma Territory in the 1890's.

Cooke, David C. *Post of honor.* **Putnam, 1958.**
Novel about an Indian uprising in 1868 that presents both sides of the red-white relationship.

Coolidge, Dane. *Gringo gold.* **Dutton, 1939.**
Story about the bandit Murrieta in California during the gold rush period.

Crabb, Richard. *Empire on the Platte.* **World, 1967.**
Good novel, with authoritative background, of the rivalry between cattlemen and homesteaders in the Platte Valley in the 1870's.

Cranston, Paul. *To heaven on horseback.* **Messner, 1952.**
A novel about Narcissa and Marcus Whitman based on the former's letters and diaries.

Croy, Homer. *Wheels west.* **Hastings, 1955.**
A novel about the tragedy of the Donner Party.

Culp, John H. *Born of the sun.* Sloane, 1959.
Long but action-filled novel of the cattle drives of Texas in the 1870's.

Culp, John. *Men of Gonzales.* Sloane, 1960.
Fictionalized story of a true bit of history — a troop of thirty-two men who rode to relieve the siege of the Alamo in 1836.

Cushman, Dan. *Silver mountain.* Appleton, 1957.
How a man achieved success in the mining fields of Montana in the late 19th century.

Davis, Clyde B. *Nebraska coast.* Farrar, 1939.
An authentic and well-written novel about frontier life in Nebraska during the 1860's.

Davis, Harold L. *Honey in the horn.* Harper, 1935.
Realistic picture of many types of people in Oregon in the first decade of the 20th century.

Davis, James F. *Road to San Jacinto.* Bobbs, 1936.
Realistic story of the Texan War for independence; good authenticity.

Dieter, William. *The white land.* Knopf, 1970.
A story of a Montana ranch during a blizzard in the 1880's, and of two men, one a fatalist and one a pragmatist.

Drago, Harry. *Montana road.* Morrow, 1935.
Good account of the opening of Dakota Territory, with Custer a prominent figure. Takes a sympathetic view of the Indian tribes.

Eckert, Allan W. *The frontiersmen.* Little, 1967.
A story of the settlement of the territory north of the Ohio, and Kentucky. Central figures are Simon Kenton and Daniel Boone. Sound history and good fiction.

Ellis, William. *Jonathan Blair.* **World, 1954.**
Good novel about a lawyer in the early West working to help settlers establish their land rights.

Emmons, Della. *Sacajawea of the Shoshones.* **Binfords & Mort, 1943.**
Fictionalized biography of the Indian woman who guided and aided Lewis and Clark.

Erdman, Loula. *Edge of time.* **Dodd, 1950.**
Pioneering in the Texas panhandle in the 1880's.

Ferber, Edna. *Cimarron.* **Doubleday, 1930.**
One of the most popular Western novels. Deals with the opening of Oklahoma to settlement.

Fisher, Vardis. *Children of God.* **Harper, 1939.**
Novel about the early days and journeys of the Mormons.

Fisher, Vardis. *City of illusion.* **Harper, 1941.**
About the Comstock Lode and Virginia City.

Fisher, Vardis. *Mountain man.* **Morrow, 1965.**
Descriptive novel of pioneer life in the Rockies in the 1830's.

Fisher, Vardis. *Tale of valor.* **Doubleday, 1958.**
Novel based on the journals of the Lewis and Clark expedition, and following them closely.

Foreman, Leonard. *Road to San Jacinto.* **Dutton, 1943.**
Adventure, good historical background and plenty of action in this story of the Texan war of independence.

Franchere, Ruth. *Stampede north.* **Macmillan, 1969.**
A 14-year old boy and his father go by steamer to the Klondike in the 1897 gold rush.

Gardiner, Dorothy. *Great betrayal.* **Doubleday, 1949.**
Good fictionalized account of the Sandy Creek massacre in Colorado
in 1864, when a cavalry troop wiped out a whole band of friendly
Indians.

Gerson, Noel. *Sam Houston.* **Doubleday, 1968.**
A biographical novel about the life of the Texas hero.

Giles, Janice. *Johnny Osage.* **Houghton, 1960.**
Set in the western country in 1821, this is about a white trader who
befriends the Osage Indians in their wars with the Cherokees, and a
young missionary girl. Good background.

Giles, Janice. *Land beyond the mountains.* **Houghton, 1958.**
Authentic and well-told story of the Kentucky frontier around 1790,
and especially about James Wilkinson, the man who tried to steal a
western empire for himself.

Giles, Janice. *Savanna.* **Houghton, 1961.**
Story of a woman's career on the frontier in Arkansas Territory
before the Civil War.

Giles, Janice. *Voyage to Santa Fe.* **Houghton, 1962.**
Good account of a group of people traveling overland from Oklahoma
to New Mexico in the late 1880's.

Gipson, Fred. *Old yeller.* **Harper, 1956.**
Pleasant story of a boy and a dog in pioneer Texas in the 1860's.

Guthrie, A. B. Jr. *Big sky.* **Sloane, 1947.**
Excellent novel of frontier life and adventure in the pioneer West
of the 1830's.

Guthrie, A. B. Jr. *Arfive.* **Houghton, 1970.**
A novel of the last years of the old West, around the turn of the
century. Set in the foothills of the Rockies.

191

Guthrie, A. B. Jr. *Way west.* **Sloane, 1949.**
Describes a wagon train journey in the 1840's from Missouri to Oregon.

Haines, William W. *The winter war.* **Little, 1961.**
Interesting and exciting novel about the army's pursuit and final defeat of the Sioux and Cheyennes in 1876 after Custer's catastrophe.

Hall, Oakley. *Warlock.* **Viking, 1958.**
Unusually good story about a western town in the 1880's, ruled by evil men, and of the efforts of moral citizens to restore honest government.

Harris, John and Margaret. *Chant of the hawk.* **Random, 1959.**
Story of mountain men and trappers in the far Northwest in the 1840's.

Haycox, Ernest. *Bugles in the afternoon.* **Little, 1944.**
Exciting story about General Custer and the Battle of the Little Big Horn.

Haycox, Ernest. *The earthbreakers.* **Little, 1952.**
Realistic novel about a group of settlers coming to Oregon in the 1840's.

Henry, Will. *No survivors.* **Random, 1950.**
Authentic novel of the Indian warfare which reached its climax at Custer's defeat.

Horgan, Paul. *A distant trumpet.* **Farrar, 1960.**
About a young army couple who are stationed at a post in Apache country in the 1880's.

Hough, Emerson. *Covered wagon.* **Appleton, 1922.**
Famous story of pioneers to California at the time of the gold rush.

Hueston, Ethel. *Man of the storm.* **Bobbs, 1936.**
Romantic novel involving the Lewis and Clark expedition and the American acquisition of Louisiana.

Jennings, John. *River to the west.* **Doubleday, 1948.**
An adventure tale about the founding of Astor's fur trading business in early Oregon.

Kantor, MacKinlay. *Spirit Lake.* **World, 1961.**
Very long and realistic novel about an 1857 massacre of white settlers by Indians. Many characters of both races are developed at length.

Kirkland, Elithe. *Divine average.* **Little, 1952.**
A novel of Texas before the Civil War, with its conflict of cultures between Mexicans and Americans.

Krause, Herbert. *Oxcart trail.* **Bobbs, 1954.**
Pioneer adventure on a settler's expedition to the Red River country in the 1850's.

Krey, Laura. *On the long tide.* **Houghton, 1940.**
Tells a story of the American settlement and conquest of Texas.

Laird, Charlton. *West of the river.* **Little, 1952.**
Good story about fur trading on the upper Mississippi in the 1830's.

Lane, Rose W. *Free land.* **Longmans, 1938.**
Describes the experiences of a young couple in the 1880's who take up land in Dakota as homesteaders. Realistic picture of the hardships.

Laughlin, Ruth. *Wind leaves no shadow.* **Whittlesey, 1948.**
Set in Santa Fe during the early 19th century, this novel centers about a real figure, a rather remarkable woman, and about the cosmopolitan life of New Mexico.

Lauritzen, Jonreed. *Rose and the flame.* **Doubleday, 1951.**
A novel of action and adventure involving Spaniards and Navajos in the Southwest around 1680.

Lea, Tom. *Wonderful country.* **Little, 1952.**
The author illustrates this book himself; it deals with Texas and Mexico in the 1880's.

Le May, Alan. *The searchers.* **Harper, 1954.**
A "western," but with good historical setting in Texas just after the Civil War.

Le May, Alan. *The unforgiven.* **Harper, 1957.**
Texas settlers defend themselves against Kiowa Indian attacks in the 1870's.

Lockwood, Sarah. *Elbow of the Snake.* **Doubleday, 1958.**
Story of a pioneer family in Idaho early in the present century.

Loomis, Noel. *Time for violence.* **Macmillan, 1960.**
Texas in the 1880's and the bitter contest between ranchers and outlaws.

Lott, Milton. *Dance back the buffalo.* **Houghton, 1958.**
Warm and sympathetic portrayal of the tragedy of the last of the Plains Indians in the 1890's.

MacDonald, Norman. *Song of the axe.* **Ballantine, 1957.**
Story of lumbering in the Pacific Northwest in the early 1900's.

Manfred, Frederick. *Lord Grizzly.* **McGraw, 1954.**
Vivid story of a mountain man in the 1820's who fought his way to safety after being savagely attacked by a bear.

Mason, Van Wyck. *End of the track.* **Reynal, 1943.**
Exciting action-filled Western about a Colorado town as the Union Pacific was being built through it.

McKee, Ruth. *Christopher Strange.* **Doubleday, 1941.**
Very long novel of a Harvard man who migrates to California in the 1850's and learns to adjust to the new conditions he finds.

McKeown, Martha. *Mountains ahead.* **Putnam, 1961.**
Wagon train journey from Missouri along the Oregon Trail in 1847.

Meigs, Cornelia. *Railroad west.* **Little, 1937.**
Romance and colorful action in the laying of track for the Northern Pacific across the prairie.

Moberg, Vilhelm. *The last letter home.* **Simon & Schuster, 1961.**
Good picture of Swedish settlers in 19th century Minnesota.

Morrow, Honore. *Beyond the blue Sierra.* **Morrow, 1932.**
About the early days of settlement in California.

Norris, Kathleen. *The Venables.* **Doubleday, 1941.**
About a family in San Francisco around the time of the earthquake, and their solidarity in the face of trouble.

O'Dell, Scott. *Hill of the Hawk.* **Bobbs, 1947.**
A story of California just before the discovery of gold. Kit Carson is an important figure.

O'Rourke, Frank. *Far mountains.* **Morrow, 1959.**
Story about a boy in New Mexico while it was still Mexican territory. Authentic and colorful.

Paul, Charlotte. *Gold mountain.* **McGraw, 1953.**
Portraits of a young school mistress and other residents of a small logging town in the Northwest in the 1880's.

Payne, Robert. *The chieftain.* **Prentice, 1953.**
About Chief Joseph and the Nez Perce Indians in the Pacific Northwest.

Pearce, Richard. *Impudent rifle.* **Lippincott, 1951.**
Set in frontier country in the 1830's, it tells how a young West Pointer fights corrupt Indian agents.

Pearce, Richard. *Restless border.* **Lippincott, 1952.**
A story of frontier action in Texas in 1839 against the Mexicans and Comanches.

Peattie, Donald C. *Forward the nation.* **Putnam, 1942.**
Story about the Lewis and Clark expedition, with emphasis on the wonders of nature in the unsettled West.

Peeples, Samuel. *Dream ends in fury.* **Harper, 1949.**
Violent story of Murrieta, the Mexican who came to California in 1849, saw his wife and his brother murdered, and turned bandit in revenge.

Portis, Charles. *True grit.* **Simon & Schuster, 1968.**
Highly enjoyable and humorous story of a young girl who in the 1880's tries to track down her father's killer in Texas and Indian Territory. One reviewer calls it "pure, beautiful corn."

Prebble, John. *Buffalo soldiers.* **Harcourt, 1959.**
Good novel about a troop of Negro cavalrymen at the end of the Civil War who undertake an exciting chase after Comanche Indians in Texas.

Prebble, John. *Spanish stirrup.* **Harcourt, 1958.**
Well-written powerful story of a western cattle drive from Texas to Kansas in the 1870's.

Putnam, George P. *Hickory shirt.* **Duell, 1949.**
Vivid story of a dangerous wagon journey across Death Valley in 1850, with two men bitterly opposed to each other as the human danger element.

Richter, Conrad. *The lady.* **Knopf, 1957.**
Good picture of violent conditions in the Southwestern frontier in the 1880's.

Richter, Conrad. *Sea of grass.* **Knopf, 1937.**
Novel portraying the conflict between cattlemen and homesteaders on the western plains of the 1880's, and the effects of plowing on the land.

Rolvaag, Ole E. *Giants in the earth.* **Harper, 1927.**
One of the finest novels of pioneer life on the Great Plains of the Dakotas in the 1880's.

Ross, Zola. *Green land.* **Bobbs, 1952.**
A story of the building of the Northern Pacific Railroad.

Sandoz, Mari. *Miss Morissa.* **McGraw, 1955.**
Story of a woman doctor in frontier Nebraska in the 1870's.

Savage, Les. *Royal city.* **Hanover, 1956.**
War and intrigue in Santa Fe during the Pueblo revolt of 1680.

Seifert, Shirley. *Those who go against the current.* **Lippincott, 1943.**
Good novel about the opening up of the Missouri River to white settlement.

Shrake, Edwin. *Blessed McGill.* **Doubleday, 1968.**
Laid in the American Southwest of the 1880's, this is a blood-curdling story of a man among Indians, villains and perpetrators of all sorts of violence.

Sinclair, Harold. *The cavalryman.* **Harper, 1957.**
Exciting story of Indian warfare in the Dakotas in the 1860's.

Stewart, George R. *East of the giants.* **Holt, 1938.**
Set in early California in the 1840's and 50's. A good picture of the place and times.

Stone, Irving. *Immortal wife.* **Doubleday, 1944.**
Biographical novel about Jessie Fremont, the wife of the explorer.

Straight, Michael. *Carrington.* **Knopf, 1959.**

Good fictional treatment of a true episode of Western history — the massacre of 81 soldiers by Sioux Indians in 1866. Carrington was the senior officer unjustly charged with the responsibility.

Straight, Michael. *A very small remnant.* **Knopf, 1963.**

A vivid story of the Sand Creek Massacre in Colorado in 1864, when an army troop nearly wiped out a Cheyenne village which had already made peace with a white commander.

Taylor, Robert. *Travels of Jamie McPheeters.* **Doubleday, 1958.**

Exciting adventures of a boy and his father as they make their way from the East to California in 1849.

Teilhet, Darwin L. *Road to glory.* **Funk, 1956.**

Pleasant and well-written story about the work of Junipero Serra with the California Indians and missions in 1783.

Ulyatt, Kenneth. *North against the Sioux.* **Prentice, 1967.**

Frontier action in this story of the siege of Fort Phil Kearney by the Sioux in 1866.

Van Every, Dale. *Scarlet feather.* **Holt, 1959.**

Adventure story set in the Kentucky frontier of the 1790's. Action and authentic detail.

Van Every, Dale. *Trembling earth.* **Messner, 1953.**

Interesting and realistic story of events in 1811 at the time of the great earthquakes in the Mississippi valley.

Van Every, Dale. *The voyagers.* **Holt, 1957.**

Picaresque novel of adventure on the Ohio and Mississippi Rivers in the 1780's. Excellent historical authenticity.

Wellman, Paul. *Comancheros.* **Doubleday, 1952.**

A story of Texas in the 1840's, with desperados, gun fights and other western staples.

Wellman, Paul. *Iron mistress.* **Doubleday, 1951.**
Action story of the early west, centering chiefly on the famous
frontiersman, Jim Bowie.

Wellman, Paul. *Magnificent destiny.* **Doubleday, 1962.**
Adventure and action are plentiful in this double-biographical story
about Andrew Jackson and Sam Houston.

Wellman, Paul. *Ride the red earth.* **Doubleday, 1958.**
Rousing adventure story of Spanish-French rivalry in the Southwest
in the early 1700's. The hero is the Chevalier de St. Denis.

White, Stewart E. *Long rifle.* **Doubleday, 1932.**
Story of a mountain man in the Rockies in the 1820's. Colorful picture of early trappers.

Williams, Mary. *Fortune, smile once more!* **Bobbs, 1946.**
Enjoyable story of an Australian convict and his girl, who escape to
California during the gold rush period.

Ziegler, Isabelle. *Nine days of Father Serra.* **Longmans, 1951.**
A story of the founder of the California missions.

JUVENILE

Adams, Samuel H. *Wagons to the wilderness.* **Winston, 1954.**
Adventures of a boy on a wagon train expedition to Santa Fe in 1822.

Allen, Merritt. *East of Astoria.* **Longmans, 1956.**
Realistic story about the earliest fur settlements in Oregon and the
British-American rivalry.

Allen, Merritt. *Make way for the brave.* **Longmans, 1950.**
Good story of a boy's adventures on the Oregon Trail in the 1830's.

Allen, Merritt. *Out of a clear sky.* **Longmans, 1938.**
Story of two boys in the 1850's who join a wagon train to California
and are involved in the Mormon Massacre at Mountain Meadows.

Allen, Merritt. *Silver wolf.* **Longmans, 1951.**
Good adventure story about Kit Carson and the Santa Fe trail in the
first half of the 19th century.

Allen, Merritt. *Spirit of the eagle.* **Longmans, 1947.**
Story of a boy who, the only survivior of an Indian raid, escapes and
joins Captain Bonneville and the Mountain Men. Good background
on early pioneering.

Annixter, Jane and Paul. *Wagon scout.* **Holiday, 1965.**
Frontier adventure story of a wagon train from the East to California
after the Civil War.

Baker, Betty. *And one was a wooden Indian.* **Macmillan, 1970.**
A story about two young Apaches' first encounter with white soldiers
in the 1850's.

Baker, Betty. *Killer-of-death.* **Harper, 1963.**
Vivid picture of the coming to manhood through trial of an Apache
boy, and of his feud with a rival youth.

Bell, Margaret. *Daughter of Wolf House.* **Morrow, 1957.**
A story for girls, set among Alaskan Indians as they first become
involved with white men.

Benet, Laura. *Hidden valley.* **Dodd, 1938.**
Boys' adventure story, exploring Yosemite while Fremont's expedition was in California.

Bolton, Ivy. *Wayfaring lad.* **Messner, 1948.**
Adventures of a boy among Indians and pioneers in the Tennessee
frontier.

Bonham, Frank. *Honor bound.* **Crowell, 1963.**
Southern boy travels to the Far West by stagecoach just before the Civil War, and becomes involved in dangerous intrigue and adventure.

Bosworth, Allan. *Ladd of the Lone Star.* **Aladdin, 1952.**
Adventure story in early Texas, involving the Alamo and the Battle of San Jacinto.

Bronson, Lynn. *Rogue's valley.* **Lippincott, 1952.**
Indian adventure in the Oregon country in the 1850's.

Bronson, Lynn. *The runaway.* **Lippincott, 1953.**
About a boy's experiences in the army in Oregon in 1848, and about Capt. U. S. Grant.

Butler, Beverly. *Fur lodge.* **Dodd, 1959.**
Adventures of a boy on a fur-trading expedition in Minnesota before its settlement.

Callahan, Lorna. *Where the trail divides.* **McGraw, 1956.**
A young girl and her father from New Orleans join a wagon train of settlers going to Oregon in pioneer days.

Caudill, Rebecca. *Far-off land.* **Viking, 1964.**
Good pioneer adventure story for girls. Flatboat travel in the West in 1780.

Caudill, Rebecca. *Tree of freedom.* **Viking, 1949.**
A story of pioneer life in Kentucky at the close of the Revolution.

Chastain, Madye. *Steamboat south.* **Harcourt, 1951.**
Story of a young girl's exciting steamboat trip from Ohio to Texas in the 1850's.

Chester, Michael. *First wagons to California.* **Putnam, 1965.**
A novel based on the writings of a member of the first expedition to go from the Middle West to California entirely by wagon train, in 1844.

Constant, Alberta. *Miss Charity comes to stay.* **Crowell, 1959.**
Pleasant story of a group of families in the Cherokee Strip of Oklahoma in the 1890's.

Derleth, August. *Empire of fur.* **Aladdin, 1953.**
Story of the fur traders around Lake Superior in the 1820's.

Downey, Fairfax. *Cavalry mount.* **Dodd, 1947.**
A lively and well-written novel of the Indian wars in Texas after the Civil War.

Downey, Fairfax. *Trail of the iron horse.* **Scribner, 1952.**
A story of the building of the Union Pacific Railroad in 1869.

Eifert, Virginia. *Buffalo trace.* **Dodd, 1955.**
Story of how Lincoln's grandfather moved into pioneer Kentucky in the 1780's, and of Lincoln's childhood there.

Erdman, Loula. *Wind blows free.* **Dodd, 1952.**
Story of a girl who learns to like the life of the Texas plains in the 1890's.

Erskine, Dorothy. *Big ride.* **Crowell, 1958.**
Story about the first colonizing expedition into California from Mexico in 1775.

Frazee, Steve. *Year of the big snow.* **Holt, 1962.**
A story of Fremont's fourth expedition in the Far West in which a 14-year old boy was actually a member.

Frazier, Neta. *Rawhide Johnny.* **Longmans, 1957.**
Boy's adventures in the Pacific Northwest in the setting of railroad building.

Frazier, Neta. *Young Bill Fargo.* **Longmans, 1955.**
The many adventures of a boy making his way to the Pacific Northwest to find his brother in 1869.

Garst, Doris. *Jim Bridger.* **Houghton, 1952.**
A biography in fiction form, with a good deal of information about trapping and the mountain men.

Garst, Warren. *Texas trail drive.* **Ariel, 1952.**
A story of the great cattle drives from Texas to Kansas in the 1870's.

Garthwaite, Marion. *Coarse Gold gulch.* **Doubleday, 1956.**
Adventures of two children in search of their father during the California gold rush.

Gendron, Val. *Fork in the trail.* **Longmans, 1952.**
Young man heads for California in 1849, but is delayed by so many obstacles that he decides he would do better to go back to Texas.

Gendron, Val. *Powder and hides.* **Longmans, 1954.**
A boy's experiences in the Plains country in 1873 while on a buffalo hunt.

Gringhuis, Richard. *Young voyageur.* **McGraw, 1955.**
Story of a farm boy who in the 1760's runs away from home to adventure among the Indians with a French trapper.

Harris, Christie. *West with the white chiefs.* **Atheneum, 1965.**
Adventures of a party of explorers crossing the Rockies in 1863.

Hawthorne, Hildegarde. *Westward the course.* Longmans, 1946.
Story of the Lewis and Clark expedition, with details centering about two boys in the party.

Howard, Elizabeth. *Girl of the north country.* Morrow, 1957.
Story for girls about a pioneer family in northern Michigan in the 1850's.

Johnson, Annabel and Edgar. *Torrie.* Harper, 1959.
Good story of a wagon train journey to California, in which a girl, resenting her parents' decision to make the trip, learns much about courage and unselfishness.

Kjelgaard, James. *Wolf brother.* Holiday, 1957.
About an Apache boy who had lived with whites for a number of years in the 1880's, but returns to help his tribe.

Lampman, Evelyn. *Cayuse courage.* Harcourt, 1970.
Interesting story of the Indian massacre in Oregon in 1847, in which Marcus Whitman died. It is told from the point-of-view of the Indians, especially one boy.

Lampman, Evelyn. *Princess of Fort Vancouver.* Doubleday, 1962.
Story of the daughter of the head of the Hudson's Bay Company post in Vancouver in the early 19th century.

Latham, Jean. *Retreat to glory.* Harper, 1965.
Fictionalized biography of Sam Houston, with good background of early Texas history.

Lathrop, West. *Keep the wagons moving!* Random, 1949.
Adventure story for boys about the Oregon Trail in the 1840's.

Lavender, David. *Golden trek.* Westminster, 1948.
Adventures of a boy on the 49'er trail to California.

Layton, Mark. *Gold prospector.* **Longmans, 1948.**
Story of a young man who goes West to look for gold in 1884. Good detail on the techniques of prospecting.

Le Sueur, Meridel. *Sparrow Hawk.* **Knopf, 1950.**
Story of a white boy and an Indian boy of the Sauks during the 1830's, when the tribe was trying unsuccessfully to hold its lands.

Means, Florence. *Rains will come.* **Houghton, 1954.**
Excellent picture of Hopi Indians in the 1880's.

Parks, Edd. *Pioneer pilot.* **Bobbs, 1947.**
A story of the earliest days of steamboating on the Ohio and the Mississippi.

Pederson, Elsa. *Dangerous flight.* **Abingdon, 1960.**
Exciting boys' adventure story set in Russian Alaska shortly before its purchase by the U. S.

Pritchett, Lulita. *Cabin at Medicine Springs.* **Watts, 1958.**
Realistic story about pioneer life in Colorado in the 1870's.

Reynolds, Dickson. *Fur brigade.* **Funk, 1953.**
Good adventure story of the Columbia River fur trade in the early 1800's.

Robinson, Barbara. *Trace through the forest.* **Lothrop, 1965.**
Story of a boy in Colonel Zane's exploring party in Ohio in 1796, and his adventures in searching for his father who had been captured by Indians.

Sackett, Rose. *Penny Lavender.* **Macmillan, 1947.**
A story for girls, about a young girl who moves from Missouri to Fort Snelling in the log cabin days of Minnesota.

Sperry, Armstrong. *River of the West.* Winston, 1952.
Good sea story dealing with Captain Gray's voyage around Cape Horn to the Pacific Northwest and his discovery of the Columbia River.

Steele, William. *Year of the bloody sevens.* Harcourt, 1963.
Exciting story of frontier life and Indian warfare in Kentucky in 1777.

Sutton, Margaret. *Palace wagon family.* Knopf, 1957.
Story about the Donner Party tragedy, based on letters of a survivor.

White, Dale. *Hold back the hunter.* Day, 1959.
Story about the first organized exploration of the Yellowstone country in 1870.

White, Dale. *Singing Boones.* Viking, 1957.
Girls' story of a Missouri family who migrate to California in the 1850's. Romance and adventure.

THE SOUTH

Basso, Hamilton. *Light infantry ball.* Doubleday, 1959.
Picture of Southern society as it was affected by slavery and the Civil War.

Bontemps, Arna. *Black thunder.* Macmillan, 1936.
About a slave revolt in Richmond in the early 1800's.

Buckmaster, Henrietta. *Deep river.* Harcourt, 1944.
Well-written if over-long novel set in Georgia just before the Civil War. The protagonists are a man with a strong feeling against slavery and secession, and his wife, raised in the customary Southern milieu.

Carr, John Dickson. *Papa Lá-bas.* **Harper, 1968.**
A mystery story set in New Orleans in 1858, and featuring Senator Judah P. Benjamin. Excellent background; equally good whodunit.

Coker, Elizabeth. *India Allan.* **Dutton, 1953.**
Novel about South Carolina from 1850 to 1876, a crucial quarter-century.

Davis, Julia. *Bridle the wind.* **Rinehart, 1953.**
Wife of a slaveowner helps a slave to escape and is in family disgrace.

Downes, Anne. *Quality of mercy.* **Lippincott, 1959.**
Story set partly in Tennessee in 1813 when Jackson was fighting the Creek Indians.

Fleishman, Glen. *While rivers flow.* **Macmillan, 1963.**
A novel depicting the struggle of the Cherokee people to keep their tribal lands in Georgia in the early 19th century.

Forrest, Williams. *Trail of tears.* **Crown, 1958.**
Portrays the tragic story of the expulsion of the Cherokees from Georgia to Oklahoma. Central figure is John Ross, half-white leader of the tribe.

Hall, Rubylea. *Great tide.* **Duell, 1947.**
A long vivid novel of life on a Florida plantation in the 1830's. Excellent background material.

Kane, Harnett. *Bride of fortune.* **Doubleday, 1948.**
Romantic fiction about the life of Varina Howell Davis, wife of the Confederacy's President.

Kendrick, Baynard. *Flames of time.* **Scribner, 1948.**
Dramatic novel of Florida in the early 1800's when it was a battle-ground among Indians, Spaniards and Americans.

Krey, Laura L. *And tell of time.* Houghton, 1938.
A long and interesting novel of the post-Civil War period in part of Texas. Depicts the effects of the war and reconstruction on the local planters.

Mally, Emma. *Abigail.* Appleton, 1956.
Romantic story of a northern girl who marries her slave-owning Virginia cousin. Good account of the Underground Railway.

Marius, Richard. *Coming of rain.* Knopf, 1969.
The setting is a Tennessee town in the 1880's, still torn by the divisive effects of the Civil War. There is drama, mystery and a cast of remarkable characters.

Markey, Gene. *That far paradise.* McKay, 1960.
Story of a Virginia family's adventures in 1794 in moving from the Blue Ridge west to Kentucky.

McMeekin, Clark. *The Fairbrothers.* Putnam, 1961.
Story about a family in Kentucky in the late 19th century. Racing and horse-breeding are their speical interests.

Myers, John. *Wild Yazoo.* Dutton, 1947.
Novel of colorful action in the early days of the Mississippi Territory.

Parrish, Anne. *Clouded star.* Harper, 1948.
Story of a young slave boy's experiences as a fugitive going North just before the Civil War. Harriet Tubman is the chief character.

Pierce, Ovid. *On a lonesome porch.* Doubleday, 1960.
Nostalgic picture of a Southern family after the Civil War trying to remake its life under very different conditions.

Pope, Edith. *River in the wind.* Scribner, 1954.
Realistic novel about the Seminole War in Florida around 1830.

Settle, Mary Lee. *Know nothing.* **Viking, 1960.**
A group of people living in "Beulah Land," now West Virginia, shortly before the Civil War.

Slaughter, Frank G. *The warrior.* **Doubleday, 1956.**
About Osceola and the Seminole wars in Florida in 1835.

Stribling, T. S. *The forge.* **Doubleday, 1931.**
Good portrayal of a small Southern town at the time of the Civil War, and of a white working-class family.

Stribling, T. S. *The store.* **Doubleday, 1932.**
Outstanding novel picturing the small Southern town in the 1880's.

Styron, William. *Confessions of Nat Turner.* **Random, 1967.**
Widely-acclaimed novel about the Negro slave who led an uprising against the whites in Virginia in 1831. Looks at slavery as a highly intelligent victim may have seen it.

Taylor, Robert L. *Journey to Matecumbe.* **McGraw, 1961.**
A sort of Huck Finn adventure tale of Davie Burnie and his Uncle Jim, who in 1870 make their way from Kentucky to the Florida Keys.

Upchurch, Boyd. *The slave stealer.* **Weybright & Talley, 1968.**
Story of an itinerant peddler in the Southern mountains before the Civil War, who aids runaway slaves to escape. In this case he helps a young and beautiful girl.

Vaughan, Carter. *The river devils.* **Doubleday, 1968.**
Set in New Orleans about 1800, a story of conflict and action between settlers and bargemen, and the French authorities.

Walker, Margaret. *Jubilee.* **Houghton, 1966.**
Story of a girl who grew up as a slave but when freedom came was determined to overcome all obstacles and have a home and family of her own.

Wilder, Robert. *Bright feather.* **Putnam, 1948.**
Action and romance in this novel of the Seminole Wars in Florida in the 1830's.

Williams, Ben Ames. *The unconquered.* **Houghton, 1952.**
A story of Louisiana politics during the post-Civil War reconstruction period. Good writing.

JUVENILE

Douglas, Marjory S. *Freedom river.* **Scribner, 1953.**
Setting is Florida in 1845, where three boys — a Negro slave, a Seminole and a white Quaker — meet problems of the meaning of freedom.

Sterling, Dorothy. *Freedom train.* **Doubleday, 1954.**
Fictionalized biography of Harriet Tubman, a leader in fighting slavery. Well-done.

THE NORTH AND EAST

Adams, Samuel H. *Canal Town.* **Random, 1944.**
Excellent portrait of an Erie Canal village (Palmyra, N. Y.) in 1820. A young doctor is the chief figure.

Aldrich, Bess Streeter. *Song of years.* **Appleton, 1939.**
Pioneer life in the Midwest in the 19th century.

Burlingame, Roger. *Three bags full.* **Harcourt, 1936.**
A chronicle of a family of 18th century Dutch New Yorkers who settled in the Finger Lakes region. The story covers a century and a half of their story and of the town they founded.

Carmer, Carl. *Genesee fever.* **Farrar, 1941.**
Well-written novel of 19th century central New York State.

Chase, Mary Ellen. *Silas Crockett.* **Macmillan, 1935.**
A well-written chronicle of four generations of a Maine family in the 19th century, beginning with the captain of a clipper ship.

Clark, Howard. *Mill on Mad River.* **Little, 1948.**
Story of a young man growing up with the brass and clock-making industries in Connecticut. Early 19th century.

Coffin, Robert P. *John Dawn.* **Macmillan, 1936.**
The ship-building industry in Maine in the 19th century.

Colver, Anne. *Listen for the voices.* **Farrar, 1939.**
A novel about Concord and its literary luminaries in the mid-19th century.

Derleth, August. *Hills stand watch.* **Duell, 1960.**
A regional novel authentically picturing the life of a Wisconsin village in the 1840's.

Duncan, Thomas W. *Big river, big man.* **Lippincott, 1959.**
Very long novel about lumbering and industrial growth in America of the mid-1880's. The careers of three go-getters are described in vivid detail.

Edmonds, Walter D. *Chad Hanna.* **Little, 1940.**
Set in New York's Mohawk Valley in the 1830's, this is the story of a runaway boy who joins a circus. Fine atmosphere and characterizations.

Edmonds, Walter D. *Erie water.* **Little, 1933.**
Good story about the building of the Erie Canal.

Edmonds, Walter D. *Rome haul.* **Little, 1929.**
Story of life along the Erie Canal in mid-19th century.

Ellis, William. *Brooks legend.* **Crowell, 1958.**
Sequel to *Bounty Lands.* This deals with the activities of a frontier doctor in the early Ohio country.

Ellis, William. *Jonathan Blair, bounty lands lawyer.* **World, 1954.**
Daily life and legal practice in early Ohio.

Forbes, Esther. *Rainbow on the road.* **Houghton, 1953.**
Pleasant and charming novel about an itinerant portrait painter in New England in the 1830's.

Forbes, Esther. *Running of the tide.* **Houghton, 1948.**
Story about Salem as a center of maritime activity in the early 19th century.

Longstreth, Thomas. *Two rivers meet in Concord.* **Westminster, 1946.**
A novel whose setting is Concord in the halcyon days of Emerson, the Alcotts and the rest. Thoreau is the principal character.

Mian, Mary. *Young men see visions.* **Houghton, 1957.**
Pleasant portrayal of a New England town and its people at the turn of the century.

Moberg, Vilhelm. *Unto a good land.* **Simon & Schuster, 1954.**
Swedish immigrants as Minnesota pioneers in the 1850's.

Mudgett, Helen. *Seas stand watch.* **Knopf, 1944.**
A story of New England sailing and trade in the years between the two wars with Britain. Good authenticity.

Orr, Myron. *Mission to Mackinac.* **Dodd, 1956.**
French and English conflicts in northern Michigan before the War of 1812.

Paradise, Jean. *Savage city.* Crown, 1955.
Realistic story of New York about 1740, when there was bitter feeling against Negroes and Catholics, and a rough population augmented by privateersmen.

Poole, Ernest. *The Nancy flyer.* Crowell, 1949.
A charming story of New England in the early 1800's, concerned chiefly with stagecoaches, inns, horses and village life.

Spicer, Bart. *The wild Ohio.* Dodd, 1953.
A story of the group of refugees from revolutionary France who settled part of the Ohio valley.

Taylor, R. S. *In red weather.* Holt, 1961.
A great fire in a New England city in 1871 is the central fact of this story involving local politicians who have neglected precautions against the catastrophe.

Van de Water, Frederic. *Wings of the morning.* Washburn, 1955.
Romance set in Vermont in 1777, involving the various contending opinions of Whigs and Tories, of New Yorkers and Vermonters. Good political portrait.

West, Jessamyn. *The friendly persuasion.* Harcourt, 1945.
Warm and pleasant set of stories about a Quaker family living in Indiana in the mid-19th century.

Wharton, Edith. *Age of innocence.* Appleton, 1920.
Classic novel of New York high society at the turn of the century.

JUVENILE

Adams, Samuel H. *Chingo Smith of the Erie Canal.* Random, 1958.
Lively adventures of a boy travelling on his own in the early 1800's, when the Canal was being built.

Brill, Ethel. *Copper country adventure.* McGraw, 1949.
Adventure story of the copper mines of upper Michigan in the mid-19th century. Good background material.

Carr, Harriett. *Valley of defiance.* **Macmillan, 1957.**
About the rent wars in the Hudson River valley in the 1840's.

Dietz, Lew. *Pines for the King's navy.* **Little, 1955.**
Story for older boys. Set in Maine in the early 1700's, it deals with the rivalry between English officials and local settlers over the great forest trees.

Dustin, Agnes. *Cabin on the Silver Tongue.* **Wilde, 1946.**
Set in New Hampshire in 1780, an adventure story.

Price, Christine. *Song of the wheels.* **Longmans, 1956.**
About a boy in upper New York State who joins in the farmers' rebellion against landlords in the early 1800's.

Tufts, Anne. *As the wheel turns.* **Holt, 1952.**
Story about the early days of manufacturing in New England, as a young English immigrant makes his way in the new textile industry.

White, Leslie. *Log jam.* **Doubleday, 1959.**
Chiefly suitable for boys or men, this is a fast-paced story about the Michigan logging camps in the 1870's.

CANADA

Altrochi, Julia. *Wolves against the moon.* **Macmillan, 1940.**
About a wealthy heir in Quebec of 1794, who gives up his prospects
to become a fur trader and eventually gains a fortune of his own.

Cather, Willa. *Shadows on the rock.* **Knopf, 1931.**
A novel of French Canada.

Costain, Thomas B. *High towers.* **Doubleday, 1948.**
Adventure and romance among the leaders of the early French
settlement of Canada.

Eaton, Evelyn. *Restless are the sails.* **Harper, 1941.**
Colorful adventures of a French prisoner in the English colonies who
escapes and makes his arduous way to Louisbourg to warn of an
impending English attack.

Elwood, Muriel. *Heritage of the river.* **Scribner, 1945.**
An adventure romance of French Canada, with Indian wars, intrigue
and violence as well as love.

Elwood, Muriel. *Web of destiny.* **Bobbs, 1951.**
A novel about Canada during the last years of French control.

Jennings, John. *Strange brigade.* **Little, 1952.**
Story about a group of Scots who, evicted from their lands, join a
Hudson's Bay Company expedition to settle Manitoba in 1813.

Lancaster, Bruce. *Bright to the wanderer.* **Little, 1942.**
A fast-moving adventure story about the Rebellion of 1837 in Upper
Canada.

Lutz, Giles A. *Magnificent failure.* **Doubleday, 1967.**
Western-type adventure set in Saskatchewan in 1884 against the background of the Riel Rebellion.

MacLennan, Hugh. *Two solitudes.* **Duell, 1945.**
Good novel which portrays in its plot and characters the still-unresolved French-English conflict of Canada.

Merrick, Elliott. *Frost and fire.* **Scribner, 1939.**
Story of the struggle of a little community in Labrador against the rigors of the climate and the fur-trading company.

Niven, Frederick. *Mine inheritance.* **Macmillan, 1940.**
Good novel giving a graphic picture of the settlement of Manitoba in 1812 by dispossessed Scottish crofters backed by the Earl of Selkirk.

Raddall, Thomas. *His Majesty's Yankees.* **Winston, 1943.**
A story of divided loyalties among the people of Nova Scotia during the American Revolution.

Raddall, Thomas. *Roger Sudden.* **Doubleday, 1945.**
French and English rivalry in 18th century Nova Scotia. Good background on colonial and Indian life.

Sullivan, Alan. *Three came to Villa Marie.* **Coward, 1943.**
A romantic triangle which shifts from Brittany to French Canada in the 17th century, with Indians and the wilderness as factors in the plot.

Vaczek, Louis. *River and empty sea.* **Houghton, 1950.**
Story of a young man in Quebec in 1670 who makes a long canoe trip to Hudson's Bay. Setting well-done.

Walker, David. *Where the high winds blow.* **Houghton, 1960.**
A long novel about a Canadian industrial tycoon in the frontier Northwest, and of two women in his life.

JUVENILE

Arnold, Elliott. *White falcon.* **Knopf, 1955.**
Fictionalized story of John Tanner who as a boy in the late 18th century was captured by Indians in Canada, and grew up to become an important member of the tribe.

Brill, Ethel. *Madeleine takes command.* **McGraw, 1946.**
Exciting story, based on fact, of how a young French-Canadian girl defended her home against Indians in her parents' absence.

Chalmers, J. W. *Red River adventure.* **St. Martin's, 1957.**
A story of Lord Selkirk's settlement of the Red River country of Canada with immigrants from Ireland and Scotland.

Coatsworth, Elizabeth. *Last fort.* **Winston, 1952.**
Good story for boys involving Indians, voyageurs and wilderness life in New France.

Garst, Doris. *John Jewitt's adventure.* **Houghton, 1955.**
Based on fact, a story about a young sailor who was the sole survivor of a shipwreck in Nootka Sound, where he was captive of the Indians for three years.

Guillot, Rene. *Boy and five huskies.* **Pantheon, 1957.**
Exciting adventure in far northern Canada.

Harris, Christie. *Raven's cry.* **Atheneum, 1966.**
Fictionalized account of the Haida Indians of the Queen Charlotte Islands off western Canada, who were virtually wiped out after contact with white men in the late 1700's.

Hays, Wilma. *Drummer boy for Montcalm.* **Viking, 1959.**
A story of the Battle of Quebec from the French point-of-view.

Mowat, Farley. *Lost in the Barrens.* **Little, 1956.**
Exciting story of two boys' struggle for survival during a winter expedition in Northern Canada.

Raddall, Thomas. *Son of the Hawk.* Winston, 1950.

Good story of action and adventure in the rather unusual setting of Nova Scotia during the American Revolution.

Ross, Margaret. *Wilderness river.* Harper, 1952.

A story of early fur-trading in western Canada.

Speare, Elizabeth. *Calico captive.* Houghton, 1957.

Based on fact, the story of a girl captured by Indians in 1754 and taken to Montreal as a slave.

Syme, Ronald. *Bay of the north.* Morrow, 1950.

Gripping story of Indian and exploring adventure in early Canada, based on the career of Pierre Radisson.

LATIN AMERICA AND THE CARIBBEAN

Allen, Dexter. *The jaguar and the golden stag.* **Coward, 1954.**
A colorful story of Aztec Mexico shortly before the coming of the Europeans.

Amado, Jorge. *Gabriela, clove and cinnamon.* **Knopf, 1962.**
Interesting story of a group of people in a section of a Brazilian city in the 1920's. Varied plots and characters.

Andrews, Robert. *Burning gold.* **Doubleday, 1945.**
An 18th century London surgeon ships on with Captain Dampier to the West Indies and has exciting and profitable experiences with the pirates there. Action and color.

Arnold, Elliott. *Time of the gringo.* **Knopf, 1952.**
Excellent novel packed with action, intrigue and realistic historical background. Setting is Sante Fe and the Southwest a few years before they became American territory.

Baggett, Samuel. *Gods on horseback.* **McBride, 1952.**
Romance and adventure in Mexico at the time of Cortez' arrival.

Baron, Alexander. *Golden princess.* **Washburn, 1954.**
Engrossing novel of Cortez' conquest of Mexico, and especially of his interpreter and aide, the Indian girl Marina.

Bartlett, Paul. *When the owl cries.* **Macmillan, 1960.**
A novel about the Mexican revolution that began in 1910 and overthrew the tyrannical hacienda system. Authentic background.

Beals, Carleton. *Taste of glory.* **Crown, 1956.**
Fictional biography of Bernardo O'Higgins, the Chilean patriot who led the revolt against Spain.

Bontemps, Arna. *Drums at dusk.* **Macmillan, 1939.**
A story of Haiti during the French Revolution when the Negro uprising was led by L'Ouverture.

Brown, Wenzell. *They called her Charity*. **Appleton, 1951.**
Violent action in the Danish West Indies in the 16th century, when they served as a refuge for pirates.

Carpentier, Alejo. *Explosion in a cathedral*. **Little, 1963.**
The career of Victor Hugues, a Frenchman who migrated to the West Indies during the French Revolution and became a revolutionary there, is the basis for this novel.

Carpentier, Alejo. *Kingdom of this world*. **Knopf, 1957.**
Well-written short novel about Haiti's revolt under Henri Christophe.

Cochran, Hamilton. *Windward passage*. **Bobbs, 1942.**
Lively story about the 1671 attack on Panama by Henry Morgan, the pirate.

Daviot, Gordon. *The privateer*. **Macmillan, 1952.**
Absorbing adventure story about the career of Sir Henry Morgan, raider of the Spanish Main.

Gavin, Catherine. *The cactus and the crown*. **Doubleday, 1961.**
Good, action-filled romance set in Mexico during the reign of Maximilian and Carlota, who play leading parts in the story.

Gorman, Herbert. *Breast of the dove*. **Rinehart, 1950.**
A novel dealing with the ill-fated Mexican ruler Maximilian and his wife Carlota.

Gorman, Herbert. *Cry of Dolores*. **Rinehart, 1947.**
A novel of peasants and a parish priest involved deeply in the beginnings of Mexico's 1810 revolt against Spain.

Gorman, Herbert. *Wine of San Lorenzo*. **Farrar, 1945.**
A view of the Mexican War as Mexicans saw it.

Green, Gerald. *The sword and the sun*. Scribner, 1953.
Very readable story about Peru in the early days of the Spanish
conquest.

Hays, Hoffman. *Takers of the city*. Reynal, 1946.
A colorful story of 16th century Mexico and of de la Casas, the
Apostle of the Indies, who tried to protect the Indians from the
conquistadors.

Heckert, Eleanor. *Muscavado*. Doubleday, 1968.
Well-written realistic novel dealing with an 18th century slave
rebellion in the Caribbean.

Jeffries, Bruce. *Drums of destiny*. Putnam, 1947.
Long but vivid novel of the Haitian slave revolt in the early 19th
century, and of Henri Christophe.

Lea, Tom. *The hands of Cantú*. Little, 1964.
Set in 16th century Mexico, the story revolves around horse rustling
and the importance of horses at that time. Very well written, and
illustrated by the author.

MacInnes, Colin. *Westward to Laughter*. Farrar, 1970.
A satirical novel about an 18th century slave revolt in the West
Indies. The style is that of Defoe and other writers of the period;
the problems parallel those of today.

Marchal, Lucien. *Sage of Canudos*. Dutton, 1954.
Interesting novel recounting a true episode in Brazil in the 1880's —
how a group of fanatics set up a so-called holy city in the back country and became a menace to the government.

Mason, Van Wyck. *Cutlass empire*. Doubleday, 1949.
Colorful account of the career of the pirate, Henry Morgan, scourge
of the Caribbean.

221

Millar, George R. *Crossbowman's story of the first exploration of the Amazon.* Knopf, 1955.
Very interesting novel about Orellana's expedition from Peru down the Amazon in 1541.

Niles, Blair. *Passengers to Mexico.* Farrar, 1943.
A novel about the ill-fated attempt by France to establish Maximilian as Emperor of Mexico.

O'Meara, Walter. *The Spanish bride.* Putnam, 1954.
Well-told story of a lovely Spanish actress who leaves Madrid to come to New Mexico in the 1700's. Excellent background.

Pollock, Alyce and Goode, Ruth. *Don Gaucho.* McGraw, 1950.
A novel full of action and excitement in Argentina in the early 19th century. Color and drama.

Roark, Garland. *Star in the rigging.* Doubleday, 1954.
Adventure and romance in the Texan Revolution against Mexico.

Rosa, Joao. *The devil to pay in the backlands.* Knopf, 1963.
Set in the Brazilian Northwest in the early 1900's, this is a story of violent conflict between outlaws and the military.

Spence, Hartzell. *Bride of the conqueror.* Random, 1954.
First-person narrative of a beautiful Spanish noblewoman in Pizarro's Peru, and her romantic problems.

Stacton, David. *A signal victory.* Pantheon, 1960.
A novel about the Mayas and their futile resistance to Spanish conquest.

Swarthout, Glendon. *They came to Cordura.* Random, 1958.
Strongly-written book about human courage. The setting is the American expedition into Mexico in 1916 in pursuit of Villa.

Teilhet, Darwin. *The lion's skin.* **Sloane, 1955.**
Story of action about William Walker, the American adventurer who led a filibustering expedition into Nicaragua shortly before the Civil War.

Terry, C. V. *Buccaneer surgeon.* **Doubleday, 1954.**
Romantic adventure on the Spanish Main in the Elizabethan period.

Traven, Bruno. *Rebellion of the hanged.* **Knopf, 1951.**
Highly graphic story of Indians in a Mexican lumber camp in 1910, revolting to join the peasants in the revolution against Diaz.

Trevino, Elizabeth de. *The fourth gift.* **Doubleday, 1966.**
Story of seven persons involved in the uprising of Mexicans in the 1920's defending the Catholic Church against government efforts to overthrow it.

Trevino, Elizabeth de. *House on Bitterness Street.* **Doubleday, 1970.**
The adventures of an Anglo-Mexican girl in the chaos of Mexico's 1910 revolution.

Uslar Pietri, Arturo. *The red lances.* **Knopf, 1962.**
In the war for independence in Venezuela (1811-1821), a story of conflict between an aristocrat and a powerful former slave.

Verissimo, Erico. *Time and the wind.* **Macmillan, 1951.**
A long family chronicle, from about 1750 to 1895, set in Brazil. A broad and colorful pageant of Brazilian history.

Wellman, Paul. *Angel with spurs.* **Lippincott, 1942.**
Adventure story of General Shelby's expedition into Mexico with a part of his defeated Confederate command just after the Civil War.

White, Leslie. *Look away, look away.* **Random, 1944.**
Adventure story about a group of Southerners who, after the Civil War, travel to Brazil to try to start a colony.

Wilder, Robert. *Wind from the Carolinas.* **Putnam, 1963.**
A six-generation family chronicle (1790-1920) of Tory sympathizers transplanted to the Bahamas, who give up cotton in favor of Civil War blockade-running and later rum running.

JUVENILE

Burlingame, Roger. *Mosquitoes in the Big Ditch.* **Winston, 1952.**
A French boy working in Panama under Dr. Gorgas sees the conquest of yellow fever.

Carse, Robert. *Great venture.* **Scribner, 1952.**
A lively story for boys about the ill-fated attempt by Scots in the late 1600's to plant a colony in Panama.

Collin-Smith, Joyce. *Jeremy Craven.* **Houghton, 1959.**
Story about an English boy whose uncle takes him to Mexico during the revolutionary years around 1912. Excellent background.

Holden, John. *Rattlesnake god.* **Day, 1959.**
Mayans in 15th century Yucatan revolt against barbarians.

Howard, Elizabeth. *Verity's voyage.* **Morrow, 1964.**
Adventures of an English girl in the West Indies in 1640.

Icenhower, Joseph. *Mr. Murdock takes command.* **Winston, 1958.**
Story of piracy and naval action around Haiti in the revolution of the late 1700's.

Kidwell, Carl. *Angry earth.* **Viking, 1964.**
Good background picture of life in pre-Columbian Mexico.

Lampman, Evelyn. *Temple of the sun.* **Doubleday, 1964.**
A story of the Aztec's efforts to resist conquest by Cortez.

Lobdell, Helen. *Golden conquest.* **Morrow, 1951.**
Story of a Spanish boy who comes to Mexico with Cortez hoping
to convert the natives.

Malkus, Alida. *Young Inca prince.* **Knopf, 1957.**
Exciting story of a boy's secret mission to spy on the enemies of the
Inca of Peru around 1450.

Newcomb, Covelle. *Black fire.* **Longmans, 1940.**
Fictionalized biography of the black king of Haiti, Henri Christophe.

Williams, Jeanne. *Mission in Mexico.* **Prentice, 1959.**
About an American boy who goes to Mexico to seek his father during
the period of Maximilian.

LIST OF PUBLISHERS

A

ABELARD
Abelard-Schuman, 6 W. 57th St., New York, N. Y. 10019

ABINGDON
Abingdon Press, 201 Eighth Ave., New York, N. Y. 10022

ACE
Ace Publishing Corp., 1120 Avenue of the Americas, New York, N. Y. 10036

APPLETON
Appleton-Century-Crofts, 440 Park Ave., S., New York, N. Y. 10016

ARIEL
Taplinger Publishing Co., 20 E. 10th St., New York, N. Y. 10003

ATHENEUM
Atheneum Publishers, 122 E. 42nd St., York, N. Y. 10017

B

BALLANTINE
Ballantine Books, Inc., 101 Fifth Ave., New York, N. Y. 10003

BINSFORDS & MORT
Binsfords & Mort, 2505 S.E. 11th Ave., Portland, Oregon 97242

BOBBS
Bobbs-Merrill Co., 4300 W. 62nd St., Indianapolis, Indiana 46268

BOUREGY
Bouregy, Thomas & Co., Inc., 22 E. 60th St., New York, N. Y. 10022

C

CAMBRIDGE U. P.
Cambridge University Press, 32 E. 57th St., New York, N. Y. 10022

CARRICK
See Lippincott

CENTURY
See Appleton

CHILMARK
See Random House

CHILTON
Chilton Book Co., 401 Walnut St., Philadelphia, Pa. 19106

COWARD
Coward-McCann, 200 Madison Ave., New York, N. Y. 10016

CREATIVE AGE
See Farrar, Straus & Giroux

CRITERION
Criterion Books, 257 Park Ave., New York, N. Y. 10010

CROWELL
Thos. Y. Crowell Co., 201 Park Ave. S., New York, N. Y. 10003

CROWN
Crown Publishers, 419 Park Ave. S., New York, N. Y. 10016

D

DAY
John Day Co., 62 W. 45th St., New York, N. Y. 10036

DELACORTE
Dell Publishing Co., 750 Third Ave., New York 10017

DIAL
Dial Press, 750 Third Ave., New York, N. Y. 10017

DODD
Dodd, Mead & Co., 79 Madison Ave., New York, N. Y. 10016

DORAN
See Doubleday

DORRANCE
Dorrance & Co., 1809 Callowhill St., Philadelphia, Pa. 19130

DOUBLEDAY
Doubleday & Co., 501 Franklin Ave., Garden City, N. Y. 11530

DUELL
Meredith Press, 1716 Locust St., Des Moines, Iowa 50303

DUTTON
E. P. Dutton & Co., 201 Park Ave. S., New York, N. Y. 10003

F

FARRAR
Farrar, Straus & Giroux, 19 Union Sq. W., New York, N. Y. 10003

FISCHER
See Ace

FOLLETT
Follett Publishing Co., 201 N. Wells St., Chicago, Illinois 60606

FUNK
Funk & Wagnalls Co., 380 Madison Ave., New York, N. Y. 10017

FUNK, WILFRED
See Funk

G

GREYSTONE
Hawthorne Books, Inc., 70 Fifth Ave., New York, N. Y. 10011

GROVE
Grove Press, 214 Mercer St., New York, N. Y. 10012

H

HAMMOND
Hammond, Inc., Hammond Bldg., Maplewood, N. J. 07040

HANOVER HOUSE
See Doubleday

HARCOURT
Harcourt Brace Jovanovitch, 757 Third Ave., New York, N. Y. 10017

HARPER
Harper & Row Publishers, Keystone Industrial Park, Scranton, Pa. 18512

HASTINGS
Hastings House, 10 E. 40th St., New York, N. Y. 10016

HOLIDAY
Holiday House, 18 E. 56th St., New York, N. Y. 10022

HOLT
Holt, Rinehart & Winston, 383 Madison Ave. New York, N. Y. 10017

HOUGHTON
Houghton Mifflin & Co., 2 Park St., Boston, Mass.

LIST OF PUBLISHERS

J

JEWISH PUBL.
Jewish Publication Society of America, 222 N. 15th St., Philadelphia, Pa.

K

KENEDY
P. J. Kenedy & Sons, 12 Barclay St., New York, N. Y. 10007

KNOPF
Alfred A. Knopf, 501 Madison Ave, New York, N. Y. 10022

L

LIPPINCOTT
J. B. Lippincott Co., E. Washington Sq., Philadelphia, Pa. 19105

LITTLE
Little, Brown & Co., 34 Beacon St., Boston, Mass. 02106

LIVERIGHT
Liveright Publishing Corp., 386 Park Ave. S., New York, N. Y. 10016

LONGMANS
See McKay, David

LOTHROP
Lothrop, Lee & Shepard Co., 105 Madison Ave., New York, N. Y. 10016

M

MACMILLAN
Macmillan Co., 866 Third Ave., New York, N. Y. 10022

MACRAE SMITH
Macrae Smith Co., 255 S. 15th St., Philadelphia, Pa. 19102

McCALL
McCall Publishing Co., 230 Park Ave., New York, N. Y. 10017

McCANN
See Coward

McGRAW
McGraw-Hill Book Co., 330 W. 42nd St., New York, N. Y. 10036

McKAY
David McKay Co., 750 Third Ave., New York, N. Y. 10017

MESSNER
See Simon & Schuster

MINTON
See Putnam

MORROW
William Morrow & Co., 105 Madison Ave., New York, N. Y.

MUHLENBURG
Muhlenburg Press, 2900 Queen Lane, Philadelphia, Pa.

N

NELSON
Thos. Nelson & Sons, Copewood & Davis Sts., Camden, N. J. 08103

NEW AM. LIB.
New American Library, 1301 Avenue of the Americas, New York, N. Y. 10019

NEW DIRECTIONS
New Directions Publishing Co., 333 Sixth Ave., New York, N. Y. 10014

NORTON
W. W. Norton & Co., 55 Fifth Ave., New York, N. Y. 10003

O

OBOLENSKY
Ivan Obolensky, 1117 First Ave., New York, N. Y. 10021

ORION
Orion Press, 125A E. 19th St., New York, N .Y. 10003

OXFORD U. P.
Oxford University Press, 200 Madison Ave., New York, N. Y. 10016

P

PANTHEON
Pantheon Books, 437 Madison Ave., New York, N. Y. 10022

PELLEGRINI & CUDAHY
See Farrar

PHILLIPS, S. G.
S. G. Phillips, Inc., 305 W. 86th St., New York, N. Y. 10024

PRENTICE
Prentice-Hall, Englewood Cliffs, N. J. 07632

PUTNAM
G. P. Putnam's Sons, 200 Madison Ave., New York, N. Y. 10016

R

RAND McNALLY
Rand McNally & Co., Box 7600, Chicago, Illinois 60680

RANDOM
Random House, 201 E. 50th St., New York, N. Y.

REGNERY
Henry Regnery Co., 114 W. Illinois St., Chicago, Illinois 60610

REYNAL
See Morrow

RINEHART
See Holt

ROY
Roy Publishers, 30 E. 74th St., New York, N. Y. 10021

S

ST. MARTINS
St. Martin's Press, 175 Fifth Ave., New York, N. Y. 10010

SCRIBNER
Charles Scribner's Sons, 597 Fifth Ave., New York, N. Y. 10017

SIMON & SCHUSTER
Simon & Schuster, 630 Fifth Ave., New York, N. Y. 10020

SLOANE
William Sloane Associates. See Morrow

STEIN & DAY
Stein & Day, 7 E. 48th St., New York, N. Y. 10017

STERLING
Sterling Publishing Co., 419 Park Ave. S., New York, N. Y. 10016

STOKES
See Lippincott

T

THOMAS
Thomas Publishing Co., 461 Eighth Ave., New York, N. Y. 10001

TRIDENT
See Simon & Schuster

TUPPER
See McKay, David

U

U. OF DENVER
University of Denver, Graduate School of Librarianship, Publications Dept., Denver, Colorado 80210

V

VANGUARD
Vanguard Press, 424 Madison Ave., New York, N. Y. 10017

VAN NOSTRAND
Van Nostrand-Reinhold Books, 450 W. 33rd St., New York, N. Y. 10001

VIKING
Viking Press, 625 Madison Ave., New York, N. Y. 10022

W

WALCK
Henry Z. Walck, 19 Union Sq. W., New York, N. Y. 10003

WALKER
Walker & Co., 720 Fifth Ave., New York, N. Y. 10019

WARNE
Frederick Warne & Co., 101 Fifth Ave., New York, N. Y. 10003

WASHBURN
See McKay, David

WATTS
Franklin Watts, 575 Lexington Ave., New York, N. Y. 10022

WESTMINSTER
Westminster Press, Witherspoon Bldg., Philadelphia, Pa. 19107

WEYBRIGHT & TALLEY
See Dutton

WILCOX
See Follett

WILDE
W. A. Wilde & Co., 10 Huron Drive, Natick, Mass. 01762

WINSTON
See Holt

WORLD
See Harcourt

WYN
See Ace

Z

ZIFF-DAVIS
Ziff-Davis, 1 Park Ave., New York, N. Y. 10016

INDEX OF AUTHORS

229

239

INDEX
AUTHORS

INDEX OF TITLES

PAGE

Comrade Venka 94
Conceived in liberty.................................... 140
Concord bridge.. 142
Concubine 56
Confessions of Nat Turner......................... 209
Conquer 113
Conqueror's wife 28
Conscience of the king............................... 26
Consort for Victoria.................................... 86
Conspiracy of women.................................. 4
Constantine 11
Constant star (Andrew) 21
Constant star (Foote) 51
Converts, The 11
Copper country adventure......................... 213
Corinthians, The 161
Cormorant's brood 128
Cornerstone, The 32
Corner that held them................................ 37
Coromandel ! 113
Coronation summer 85
Corsair 157
Cossacks, The 66
Cotton road 169
Council of Egypt... 84
Count Belisarius 111
Count Bohemund 26
Countess Angelique 129
Courts of love.. 22
Covenant 118
Covenant with death................................... 92
Covered wagon 192
Cow Neck rebels.. 150
Crimson is the eastern shore..................... 160
Crippled splendour 30
Crisis, The 168
Croatan 129
Cromwell's head 149
Crossbowman's story of the first
    exploration of the Amazon.................... 222
Crossing, The 139
Crown and the shadow................................ 54
Crumbling fortress 98
Cry and the covenant.................................. 64
Cry of Dolores 220
Culper spy ring.. 150
Cumberland Rifles 156
Cunning of the dove.................................... 26
Cup, the blade or the gun.......................... 169
Curtain's at eight.. 88
Cutlass empire 221

D

Daishi-san 113
Dance back the buffalo............................... 194
Dance for a diamond star........................... 70
Dancer in darkness...................................... 63
Dangerous flight 205
Dangerous spring 107
Danger to windward 122
Dara, the Cypriot.. 17
Dark angel 114
Dark hills to westward 188
Dark island 11
Dark moment 110
Darkness and the dawn............................7, 24
Darkness at noon... 93
Darkness over the land................................ 109
Dark rose 65
Dark stranger 49
Dark torrent of Glencoe.............................. 53
Daughter of Jairus 16
Daughter of time 36
Daughter of Wolf House 200
David's stranger 18
David the king 18
Dawn at Lexington...................................... 150
Dawn's early light....................................... 152
Dawn wind 44
Day must dawn 147
Day of battle (Sheean) 62

PAGE

Day of battle (Van de Water)................... 147
Day of the bomb 115
Days of danger... 68
Day without end 184
Dead are mine.. 104
Deadly lady of Madagascar........................ 119
Deadly patrol 110
Dear and glorious physician...................... 14
Death comes for the archbishop................ 187
Debbie of the Green Gate........................... 67
Deceivers, The 113
Dedicated, The 77
Deep are the valleys.................................... 23
Deep river 206
Deep six 182
Deer cry, The 35
Demelza 78
Desert harvest 180
Désirée 84
Destiny of fire.. 33
Detached command 163
Devil's rainbow 156
Devil to pay in the backlands.................... 222
Devil water 62
Dingle War 96
Diplomatic diversions 94
Discourse with shadows.............................. 102
Disinherited, The 91
Distant trumpet 192
Divine average 193
Doc Dudley's daughter................................ 179
Doctor Zhivago 94
Don Gaucho 222
Doniphan's ride 159
Do not go gentle.. 183
Don Pedro and the devil............................. 123
Don't tread on me....................................... 143
Double quest 44
Down the long stairs 67
Down the mast road 134
Dragon in New Albion................................ 125
Dragonship 125
Drawbridge gate 40
Dream ends in fury..................................... 196
Drumbeat 82
Drummer boy for Montcalm....................... 217
Drummer of Vincennes 151
Drums 138
Drums along the Mohawk........................... 139
Drums at dusk 219
Drums of destiny 221
Drums of Khartoum 118
Drums of Monmouth 146
Drums of morning 174
Dwarf, The 30

E

Eagle and the rock....................................... 86
Eagle in the sky 144
Eagle in the sun 186
Eagle of Niagara 148
Eagle of the ninth....................................... 13
Eagle of the sea 164
Eagles fly west 185
Eagles of malice 118
Earl's falconer 47
Earthbreakers, The 192
Earthshaker 118
Easter dinner 96
East Indiaman 113
East of Astoria 199
East of the giants 197
Echo of the flute.. 143
Edge of time... 190
Egyptian, The 1
Egyptian adventures 2
Egypt's Queen Cleopatra............................ 2
Eight April days.. 169
Eighty-seven days 89
Elbow of the Snake...................................... 194
Eleanor the queen 42